Albert Schmitz

Englisch Aufbaukurs Technik

ARBEITSBUCH

Max Hueber Verlag

Aufbau des Lehrwerks

Englisch – Grundkurs Technik
2181
Handbuch mit Schlüssel zu den Übungen 2.2181
Arbeitsbuch 6.2181
Schallplatten mit Aufnahmen der Lektionstexte 3.2181
Compact-Cassette mit Aufnahmen der Lektionstexte 5.2181
Tonbänder und **Compact-Cassetten** mit Aufnahmen der Lektionstexte mit und ohne Nachsprechpausen 4.2181 bzw. 9.2181
Lernwörterbuch 8.2181
Sprechübungen (in Vorbereitung)

Englisch – Aufbaukurs Technik
2189
Handbuch mit Schlüssel zu den Übungen 2.2189
Arbeitsbuch 6.2189
Compact-Cassette mit Aufnahmen der Lektionstexte 5.2189
Tonbänder und **Compact-Cassetten** mit Aufnahmen der Lektionstexte mit und ohne Nachsprechpausen 4.2189 bzw. 9.2189
Lernwörterbuch 8.2189 (in Vorbereitung)

Henry G. Freeman, Technisches Taschenwörterbuch Deutsch-Englisch 6212
Henry G. Freeman, Technisches Taschenwörterbuch Englisch-Deutsch 6213
Hans G. Hoffmann, Englische Taschengrammatik 2185

Falls das vorliegende Buch im Rahmen der Lernmittelfreiheit ausgeliehen wird, sind jegliche Eintragungen untersagt.

1. Auflage

3. 2. 1. | Die letzten Ziffern
1983 82 81 80 79 | bezeichnen Zahl und Jahr des Druckes.
Alle Drucke dieser Auflage können nebeneinander benutzt werden.
© 1979 Max Hueber Verlag München
Satz und Druck: Georg Appl, Wemding · Printed in Germany
ISBN 3-19-06.2189-6

Inhaltsverzeichnis

Hinweise für den Einsatz des Arbeitsbuchs 4

1 Brain-storming: Some more questions 6	16 Briv–high-speed riveting . 36
2 How to choose speakers . 8	17 Mathematics for fun (II) . 38
3 CONDEEP – production platform and power station 10	18 BD-5J specifications . . . 40
4 Fundamental electronics . 12	19 The pleasure of driving . . 42
5 Microwave ovens: Questions and answers 14	20 Qualified draughtsmen wanted 44
6 Another look at Nyltite seals 16	21 Fiesta facts and figures . . 46
7 A transmittal 18	22 NASA facilities: Solar heating and cooling systems 48
8 Hovercraft: Some more facts and figures 20	23 Space age shooting gallery 50
9 CB radios: Accessories and specifications 22	24 From the compressor parts list 52
10 APU 24	25 Controlling cockroaches automatically 54
11 A crossword puzzle . . . 26	26 X-ray tire inspection . . . 56
12 Electric arc furnaces . . . 28	27 Mathematical signs, symbols and operations 58
13 The bridge is breaking up! 30	28 NASA: Projects in space . 60
14 Mathematics for fun (I) . . 32	29 . . . and progress on earth . 62
15 Computer games 34	30 A digital watch kit 64
	FINAL TEST 66

Schlüssel zu den Übungen und Tests 72

Alphabetisches Wortschatzregister 81
Erklärung der Lautschrift 83

Quellenverzeichnis 84

Hinweise für den Einsatz des Arbeitsbuchs

■ Funktion des Arbeitsbuchs

Das Arbeitsbuch zum *Aufbaukurs Technik* dient in erster Linie der Vertiefung und Erweiterung des im Klassenunterricht Gelernten, und zwar für die eigenständige, häusliche Arbeit. Der Kursteilnehmer kann in dem ihm genehmen Arbeitsrhythmus unterrichtsbegleitende Übungen und Zusatztexte durcharbeiten und hat überdies durch den im Anhang vorhandenen Schlüssel die Möglichkeit einer sofortigen Erfolgskontrolle. Durch das Arbeitsbuch erhält der Kursteilnehmer die Gelegenheit, individuelle Lernschritte zu vollziehen.
Darüber hinaus eignet sich das Arbeitsbuch auch als Begleitmaterial im Klassenunterricht, da es zusätzliche Übungsmöglichkeiten bietet. Besonders wertvoll sind die Zusatztexte, die immer in einem mehr oder weniger engen Zusammenhang mit den Lehrbuchtexten stehen.

■ Lernhilfen

Es empfiehlt sich, vor dem Durcharbeiten der Übungen dieses Arbeitsbuchs noch einmal den Text der entsprechenden Lektion des Lehrbuchs durchzulesen und eventuell die Tonmaterialien einzusetzen (Cassetten oder Tonbänder). Danach sollte das Lehrbuch allerdings geschlossen werden und während der Arbeit mit den entsprechenden Übungen des Arbeitsbuchs auch geschlossen bleiben.
Nachschlagen im Schlüssel sollte man immer erst dann, wenn man eine Übung komplett fertig hat bzw. wenn man wirklich nicht mehr auf die richtige Lösung kommt.
Wiederholung kann auch hier nicht schaden: Wenn man mit einer bestimmten Übung Schwierigkeiten hatte, so ist es nützlich, sie nach einer längeren Pause noch einmal zu machen. Auf diese Art und Weise kann man feststellen, ob man sie jetzt besser beherrscht.
Beim Durcharbeiten der Übersetzungsübungen und einiger schriftlicher Übungen muß man sich vor Augen halten, daß die im Schlüssel angegebenen Lösungsvorschläge oft nicht die einzigen Lösungsmöglichkeiten sind. Im Zweifelsfalle wendet man sich am besten an den Kursleiter.

■ Hauptsächliche Übungstypen

1. Definitionsübungen: Im wesentlichen handelt es sich hier um Zuordnungsübungen, d. h. die zutreffende Definition ist dem richtigen Wort zuzuordnen. Durch derartige Übungen soll der Lernende angeregt werden, weitere Definitionen ihm unbekannter Wörter im Wörterbuch (englisch-englisch) nachzuschlagen.

2. Einsetzübungen: Es sind Sätze oder Satzteile zu vervollständigen, indem man in die Lücken ein passendes Wort oder einen passenden Ausdruck einsetzt. Die einzusetzenden Elemente sind häufig vorgegeben. Oft stehen diese Einsetzübungen in Zusammenhang mit Kurztexten oder -dialogen.

3. Strukturübungen: Sie dienen dem Einüben grammatikalischer Strukturen und haben gewöhnlich die Form einer Umwandlungs- oder Frage-und-Antwort-Übung.

4. Verständnisübungen: Es werden Fragen zu Illustrationen oder Texten gestellt, die das sinngemäße Verstehen üben und abtesten sollen.

5. Übersetzungsübungen: Diese Übungen dienen dazu, wichtige Strukturen zu üben bzw. zu wiederholen, indem sie die grammatikalischen Problemstellen bewußt machen.

6. Auswahlübungen: Hier handelt es sich um Übungen, bei denen der Kursteilnehmer entscheiden muß, welche der angebotenen Möglichkeiten die beste bzw. die richtige ist.

■ Illustrationen

Es wurde versucht, möglichst viele Illustrationen in den Übungsbereich einzubeziehen bzw. sie so auszuwählen, daß sie zur Erläuterung des Textes in optimaler Weise beitragen. Darüber hinaus findet man zahlreiche Karikaturen, die im wesentlichen der Auflockerung dienen, jedoch in vielen Fällen auch neuen Wortschatz einführen.

1 Brain-storming: Some more questions

1 Please complete the brain-storming questions below by putting in the following words:

another, attractive, economically, faster, necessary, same, single

⑬ Could it be made of _____ (and cheaper) material?

⑭ Could we have another of our products made at the _____ time as this one – thus saving cost?

⑮ Must the product have the same strength and durability *all the way through?*

⑯ Why all this packing – is it all _____?

⑰ Does the product look _____ enough?

⑱ Let's go over every _____ inch of the product and ask, "Why is this necessary?"

⑲ Is our company's name anywhere on it?

⑳ Why can't it move _____?

㉑ Are we doing anything with the product that the supplier can do more _____ for us?

㉒ Could it operate more smoothly?

2   Please put in "get used", "got used" or "used":

> **New words and phrases:**
> **operate more smoothly** ['smu:ðli] weicher (= ruhiger) arbeiten
> **packing** ['pækiŋ] Verpackung
> **all the way through** an jeder Stelle
> **single** ['siŋgl] einzeln; Einzel-; einzig
> **go over every single inch** jedes einzelne Inch durchgehen (= prüfen)
> **supplier** [sə'plaiə] Zulieferer; Lieferant

a. At first I didn't like brain-storming sessions very much but after a while I _____ to them.   b. I wonder whether he'll ever _____ to speaking English.   c. I'm sure they'll _____ to the new SI units.   d. I knew it would be difficult to drive in England since I'm not _____ to driving on the wrong side of the road.   e. She's quite _____ to brain-storming sessions since she's been working in our company for more than ten years.   f. She told me she _____ to warm beer when she was in England last year.   g. I wonder why they can't _____ to working with scrap materials from time to time. It would be much more economical.   h. They quickly _____ to the new working methods, didn't they?

3   Please complete the short dialogues below by putting in the correct questions according to the example:

> I talked to the chief engineer about that problem we're having with the computer. – And when _____ ? – Yesterday morning. . . . And when *did you talk to him?* . . .

a. She bought some new spark plugs yesterday morning. – And how many _____ ? – Five.   b. Who was there at the meeting last Monday? – Well, Mr Eaton was there, of course, and Mr Baldwin, too. Mr Eaton told me he's from Hull. – Is he? And Mr Baldwin? Where _____ ? – From London, as far as I know.   c. Our technician managed to get the machine working again. – How _____ ? – Well, he replaced a few parts, and everything was okay.   d. The chief engineer wasn't interested in what I told him about the new milling machine. – And why _____ ? – They probably don't want to buy a new milling machine.   e. She told me she's going to London next week? – And why _____ ? – I don't know.

2 How to choose speakers

1 Please put in "about", "after", "by", "in", "of", "to", "with" or "without":

"Now this is Mr. Bevis, he's our sound expert."

a. The choice _____ speaker systems is rather difficult because the manufacturer's specifications say very little _____ the character _____ the sound.

b. The ideal speaker, of course, would reproduce the entire sound range _____ adding or subtracting anything, but such a loudspeaker has never been and never will be designed.

c. When buying speaker systems, the specifications should be used _____ determine the general size, type and power range, but the final choice must be made either _____ listening tests – preferably _____ your own amplifier and _____ your own room – or, if that is impossible, _____ simply trusting a good manufacturer.

d. Speaker switch

_____ some amplifiers, you can connect two or three pairs _____ speakers which can be used separately or _____ pairs.

e. Level controls

The level control is a device which makes it possible _____ change the medium and high sound ranges _____ a certain extent.

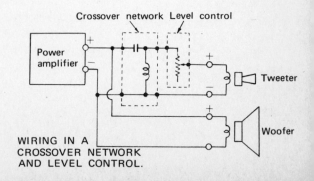

WIRING IN A CROSSOVER NETWORK AND LEVEL CONTROL.

2 Please find the correct form (e.g. buy, bought or have bought) according to the example:

> You shouldn't (buy) that old car when you were in London last week. – You shouldn't have bought that old car when you were in London last week.

New words and phrases:

speakers = loudspeakers
expert ['ekspə:t] Fachmann; Experte
choice [tʃɔis] Auswahl; Wahl
character ['kæriktə] Wesen; Charakter; Natur
ideal [ai'diəl] ideal
reproduce [ri:prə'dju:s] wiedergeben; reproduzieren
sound range Klangbereich
power range Leistungsbereich
trust [trʌst] Vertrauen; vertrauen
separate ['seprit] separat; getrennt
level control Höhen- und Tiefeneinstellung
mid range [mid] Mittelton (= Mitteltonlautsprecher)
to a certain extent bis zu einem gewissen Grade
turn down leiser stellen

a. Why didn't you (talk) to the technician before repairing the generator? – Well, I didn't (know) where he was. **b.** I (tell) him I couldn't (attend) the brain-storming session next Monday. **c.** They wouldn't (use) metal if they had known that plastics are much cheaper. **d.** He (find) the screwdriver under that old box on the workbench. **e.** You should have used a paint finish. It might (prevent) corrosion and rust.

3 Please put in "do", "did" or "have done":

a. I wonder what he would _____ if he hadn't found the leaflets with the specifications. **b.** Why don't they like the new TV appliances? – But they _____ like them. They just think they're too expensive. **c.** When _____ he tell you that he wants to build a loudspeaker himself? – Yesterday evening. **d.** _____ he explain to you what a Dolby system is? – Yes, he _____. – And when _____ he _____ that? – Last Wednesday. – Well, he should _____ that much earlier. **e.** I _____ a bit of reading last week.

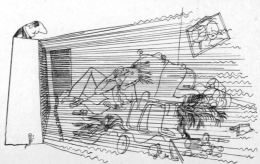

"Shall I turn it down a bit?"

3 CONDEEP – production platform and power station

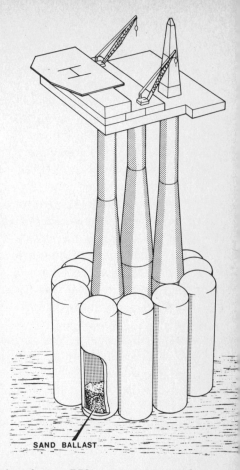

1 Please put in "bbl", "ft", "km", "m", "MV" or "MW":

a. Utilizing gas found in offshore oil fields often proves difficult. In the last few years, however, new methods have been tried, and the new technical know-how has made it possible to solve some of these problems. Two high-voltage cables (each with a capacity of about 350 _____) were laid between Denmark and Norway, a distance of approximately 130 _____, with water depths up to 550 _____ (1800 _____). New cable-laying techniques make it possible to lay up to 160 _____ of cable in 24 hours.

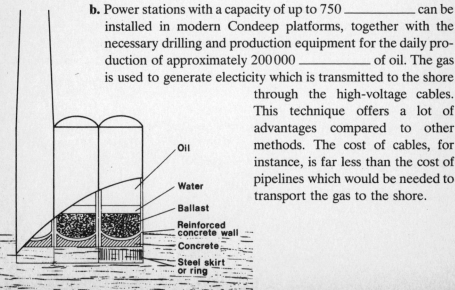

b. Power stations with a capacity of up to 750 _____ can be installed in modern Condeep platforms, together with the necessary drilling and production equipment for the daily production of approximately 200 000 _____ of oil. The gas is used to generate electicity which is transmitted to the shore through the high-voltage cables. This technique offers a lot of advantages compared to other methods. The cost of cables, for instance, is far less than the cost of pipelines which would be needed to transport the gas to the shore.

2 Please answer:

> We don't make construction platforms of concrete. – But construction platforms are often made of concrete.

a. We don't build the drilling platforms in a dry dock. **b.** We don't use aluminium for window frames. **c.** We don't include a cross-over network in the loudspeaker kit. **d.** We don't cover the machine parts with a paint finish. **e.** We don't use a computer for such jobs.

3 Please put in "to" where necessary:

a. He's attended _____ a lot of brain-storming sessions in his life.
b. The insulation material can be used for temperatures up _____ 850 °F.
c. Sixteen of the cylindrical cells _____ provide an oil storage volume of one million barrels while the other three _____ form the bases of the columns. **d.** What happens when coal is _____ heated?

4 Please put in "what" or "which":

a. I'm not sure _____ they want to do with all the computers they bought. **b.** A Dolby is an electronic system _____ reduces noise on tape and circuit. **c.** I showed him the two cross-over networks but he didn't tell me _____ of them he wanted. **d.** I wonder _____ she needs the glass wool for. **e.** Have you seen _____ they charge for the new hi-fi loudspeakers? – Yes, about two hundred pounds. **f.** The insulation system is supplied in one-piece sections _____ are very easy to install. **g.** When you read the leaflets we sent you you will see very clearly _____ the machine can be used for.

New words and phrases:

bbl = barrels (1 barrel = ca. 159 l)
MV = megavolt
MW = megawatt
utilize ['juːtilaiz] verwerten; ausnutzen
prove [pruːv] sich herausstellen als; beweisen
know-how ['nəuhau] Know-how, Sachwissen, Fachwissen
Denmark ['denmɑːk] Dänemark
Norway ['nɔːwei] Norwegen
lay [lei] (laid [leid] – have laid) legen
to the shore ans Ufer, an die Küste
transport [træns'pɔːt] transportieren; befördern
reinforced [riːinˈfɔːst] verstärkt
reinforced concrete Stahlbeton; Eisenbeton
skirt [skəːt] Rand; Saum; Rock

3

4 Fundamental electronics

1 Please find the correct explanation:

Electrical **resistance** ...
    a) ... varies with temperature.
    b) ... is always the same.

A **resistor** is used to ...
    a) ... change dc into ac.
    b) ... introduce known resistance into a circuit.
    c) ... keep the voltage low.

Wow is ...
    a) ... an alteration of current.
    b) ... low-frequency modulation caused by speed variations in record players.

An **integrated circuit** is ...
    a) ... a source of alternating current of any frequency.
    b) ... a group of electronic circuit elements put together.

Soldering means ...
    a) ... hot joining of metals by using an alloy as a thin film between the parts to be joined.
    b) ... joining pieces of metal by raising the temperature at the joint.

Hertz (abbreviation Hz) is an SI unit which indicates ...
    a) ... the number of cycles per second.
    b) ... the number of frequency modulations per second.

2 Please complete:

"Where did you get your technical training?" – He asked me where I had got my technical training.

New words and phrases:

vary ['vɛəri] variieren; (sich) verändern
introduce [intrə'djuːs] einführen; vorstellen
alteration [ɔːltə'reiʃən] Änderung
element ['elimənt] Element; Bestandteil
at the joint [dʒɔint] an der Verbindungsstelle
a thin film [film] ein dünner Film (= Schicht)
awful ['ɔːful] schrecklich
awfully sorry es tut mir schrecklich leid
short circuit Kurzschluß

a. "What do you need the leaflets for?" – She wanted to know ....

b. "Will there be any practical work?" – He asked me whether ....

c. "Why don't you study electronics at home?" – She wanted to know ....

d. "Are you interested in a new loudspeaker?" – He wanted to know ....

e. "What do you have to learn for your fundamental electronics course?" – She asked me ....

3 Please put in "for", "in" or "to":

a. He didn't get admitted _____ college last year. **b.** They will send you equipment _____ measuring various things. **c.** "Wow" is used _____ connection with turntables and tape speeds. **d.** A technician is a person who is skilled _____ the technical methods of a particular job or a particular subject.

"Awfully sorry – a short circuit!"

5 Microwave ovens: Questions and answers

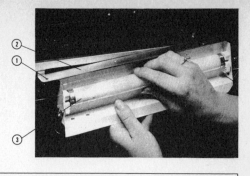

1 Please put in the following words and figures:

> assembly, cavity, finish, fluorescent, interior, items, kind, meat, rotation, shops, speed, stirrer, tube – 1, 2, 3, 13, 140

- **How do I replace burned-out lights?** 1. Remove the two screws holding the lamp _____ (see item _____ in the figure above). 2. Pull lamp assembly (item _____ above) up slightly and forward to remove. 3. Remove _____ lamp (item _____ above). Replace with new one (_____ watts), available in most _____. 4. Replace lamp assembly by sliding into opening and replace the two screws. When the microwave oven is turned on, the interior light will come on automatically.

- **What is that three-bladed fan at the top?** It is called a "_____". It helps to distribute the microwaves inside the food _____. It rotates at approximately _____ revolutions per minute. This _____ makes the _____ lights appear to flicker.

- **How much faster is microwave cooking than conventional cooking?** The _____ varies considerably with the size and _____ of food. Between six and eight pounds of _____ require about $1/4$ the time of oven roasting. Other _____ require from $1/2$ to about $1/10$ the time. Very small items, however, may become hot in as little as $1/50$ of the time needed in conventional ovens.

- **Will I damage my microwave oven if I turn it on empty?** No, but you should not do this. The magnetron _____ will not be damaged, but if the oven is allowed to remain on while empty, you may damage the interior _____.

2 Right or wrong (R or W)? Please mark the correct answer:

	R	W
a. Radio waves and microwaves have the same wave lengths.	☐	☐
b. One of the frequencies used for cooking is 2,450 Mhz.	☐	☐
c. The opening at the top is called a "stirrer".	☐	☐
d. Glass must not be used since it reflects microwaves.	☐	☐

New words and phrases:

fluorescent lamp [fluə'resnt] Leuchtstofflampe
blade [bleid] Flügel; Schaufelrad
fan [fæn] Ventilator; Gebläse
rotate [rəu'teit] (sich) drehen; rotieren
rotation [rəu'teiʃən] Drehung; Rotation
appear [ə'piə] erscheinen; sich zeigen
they appear to flicker sie scheinen zu flackern
considerable [kən'sidərəbl] beträchtlich; erheblich

3 Please put in "the" where necessary:

a. _____ microwaves are a particular frequency and _____ wave length of _____ electro-magnetic energy. b. _____ computerized traffic control system developed in Germany uses _____ variable highway signs. c. Friction produces _____ heat.

4 Please complete the following dialogues:

a. What's the technician doing? – He's repairing the motor. – How long .... repairing it now? – ...... almost an hour.

b. What's Joan doing? – She's waiting ...... the chief engineer. – How long .... for him now? – ..... eight o'clock.

c. What's the chief engineer doing? – .... the new milling machine. – How long has he been checking it now? – ...... half an hour.

d. What's Mr Eaton doing in the workshop? – He's talking to the technicians. – How long .... to them? – ...... he came to the office at nine o'clock this morning.

e. What's Jeff doing? – He's programming the computer. – .... ? – ..... early this morning.

6 Another look at Nyltite seals

1. Please use words from the drawings on the right to complete the following sentences:

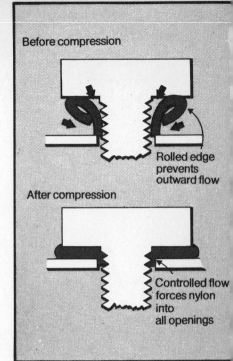

a. An interesting feature of Nyltite seals is the _____ .

b. After _____ , Nyltite seals provide a pressure- and vibration-proof seal because the _____ is forced to flow in one direction only: into the threads and between the hole and the screw shank.

c. Thus, there will be no _____ _____ of the nylon.

2. Please find the correct form of the words in brackets according to the example:

> Oh, you've got a new car? – Well, it's not really new. I (have) for eight months already. (= ... *I've had it* ...)

a. When did you move to London? – Last year, in April. – Oh, then you *(live)* there for more than a year already!   b. Do you know Mr Baldinger? – Oh yes, I know him very well. – How long *(know)* him? – Well, I first met him in Birmingham two years ago.   c. Have you assembled the conveyors yet? – No, we haven't. We're still waiting for the steel sections. – How long *(wait)* for them now? – Over a week.   d. Is Mrs Franklin in the workshop? – No, she isn't. I *(not see)* her since I arrived here this morning.   e. Have you ever been to the United States? – No, I haven't. I *(always want)* to go there but somehow I never got the chance. – Well, I *(never be)* there, either.

6

3 Please put in "about", "for" or "of":

a. Did he tell you what the meeting last Friday was _____? – No, he didn't. **b.** You should ask the English engineers what the sections for the conveyors are made _____. **c.** I wonder what they're going to talk _____ at the brain-storming session next week. **d.** What are you looking _____? – I'm looking _____ the minutes... Oh yes, here they are. **e.** Leaflets in English? No, they won't do, I'm afraid. German leaflets – that's what our customers are going to ask _____, I'm sure.

New words and phrases:

edge [edʒ] Ecke; Kante; Schneide
rolled edge aufgerollte Kante
pressure-proof druckfest
vibration [vaɪˈbreɪʃən] Erschütterung; Vibrieren; Zittern
vibration-proof erschütterungsunempfindlich
force (er)zwingen; treiben; forcieren
outward [ˈautwəd] nach (dr)außen gerichtet
controlled flow geregelte (= gelenkte) Bewegung
move *(hier:)* umziehen
have just come through sind gerade durchgekommen
fire entlassen, "feuern"
somehow irgendwie

4 Please put in "many" or "much":

a. When certain sections of the highway are carrying too _____ traffic, the computer changes the traffic signs. **b.** They've been experimenting with that system for _____ years now. I wonder how _____ it will cost us in the end. **c.** How _____ detectors do they need for collecting data? – I don't know. You'll have to ask the engineers who are building the system.

"The computer forms have just come through – you were fired fourteen months ago!" ▷

7 A transmittal

Transmittal

To/An: Mr G Lawrence

Action required by/Termin:

Remarks/Bemerkungen:

Please have a look at the minutes (see enclosure).

I would like to get them typed tomorrow and sent to Mr Baldinger.

Yours,

Kirk

- [ ] See me / Rücksprache
- [ ] Call me / Anruf
- [ ] For information / Kenntnisnahme
- [ ] For file / Ablage
- [ ] Handle / Durchführung
- [ ] Comment / Stellungnahme
- [ ] Investigate / Untersuchung
- [ ] Pass on / Weiterleitung
- [ ] Reply – my signature / Antwort – meine Unterschrift
- [ ] Reply – copy to me / Antwort – Kopie an mich
- [x] Return / Rückgabe
- [x] Approve / Genehmigung

Name: Kirk Jasper

Mail symbol/Postzeichen: LK - 662

Tel.: 4890

Date/Datum: September 2, 1978

1 Please use these words from the transmittal on the opposite page to complete the following sentences:

> approve(d), call(ed), get (got), handle(d), investigate(d), reply (replied), return(ed), type(d)

New words and phrases:

transmittal [trænz'mitl] Mitteilung
action ['ækʃən] *(hier etwa:)* Erledigung
remark Bemerkung
enclosure [in'kləuʒə] Anlage
type [taip] mit der Maschine schreiben, tippen
file [fail] Ablage; ablegen; *(auch:)* Feile; feilen
comment ['kɔment] Anmerkung; Kommentar; Anmerkung(en) machen; kommentieren
investigate [in'vestigeit] untersuchen; prüfen
pass on [pɑːs] weitergeben; weiterleiten
mail [meil] Post(sendung)
date [deit] Datum

a. Although I told them it was urgent, I had to wait for two weeks until they _____ to my letter. **b.** She _____ me from London yesterday. **c.** I showed him the new designs but he said they would have to be _____ by the chief engineer. **d.** Our conveyors can _____ all sorts of products. **e.** You should have _____ the engine checked before installing it. **f.** After an accident, the most important thing is to _____ the causes so that a similar accident will not happen again. **g.** I haven't seen her since she _____ from Birmingham last Tuesday. **h.** You should get the minutes _____ as soon as possible because I want to send them to Germany.

2 Please complete the following sentences:

a. I wonder why they don't reply _____ my letter. **b.** Do you think you can supply _____ time? – Oh yes, we certainly can. **c.** _____ impact, the plastic material is extruded from the two devices. **d.** We can supply the steel sections _____ metric sizes, too. **e.** He said the track sections were made _____ lengths _____ ten feet.

"Oh no! It wants to join a union!"

8 Hovercraft: Some more facts and figures

1. **Please find the word in the diagram below which means . . .**

   SR.N4 HOVERCRAFT. Overall length: 39.68 m (130 ft 2 in); capacity: 37 cars and 282 passengers; speed: in excess of 60 knots.

   a. . . . an opening for something; a way in.
   b. . . . a device for compressing the air supply to a turbine or jet.
   c. . . . anything burned to give heat or to operate an engine.
   d. . . . a kind of engine operated by the pressure of water, steam, air, or hot gases.
   e. . . . mixture of gases, mostly oxygen and nitrogen, surrounding the earth; atmosphere.
   f. . . . a transmission, as in a car or a lorry.
   g. . . . anything used to move air around.
   h. . . . a machine that develops power to run other machines.

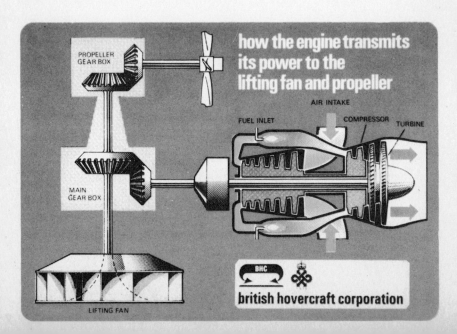

8

2 Please put in "if", "that", "when", or "which":

> **New words and phrases:**
> **knot** [nɔt] Knoten (= 1 Seemeile pro Stunde: 1.15 mph, 1.85 km/h)
> **mostly** ['məustli] hauptsächlich; größtenteils
> **lifting fan** = lift fan
> **fuel inlet** ['inlet] Brennstoff-Einlaßöffnung
> **air intake** ['inteik] Luftansaugstutzen

a. Mr Mills didn't think _____ leaflets in German were really necessary. **b.** Mr Baldinger, however, told them _____ it would be a lot easier to sell their products in Germany _____ they could give the customers information material in German. **c.** The first hovercraft used a simple chamber through _____ air was fed to form an air cushion under the craft. **d.** British Rail Hovercraft is one of the companies _____ use hovercraft for crossing the English Channel. **e.** The skirts make life more comfortable for the passengers _____ conditions are rough. **f.** The skirts, _____ were developed later on, also act as shock absorbers.

3 Please make sentences:

> design a new transmission – I can't design a new transmission. You'll have to get it designed by somebody else, I'm afraid.

a. check the lift fan **b.** type the minutes **c.** explain the conveyor system **d.** translate the English leaflets **e.** repair the gas turbine

4 Please put in "had been" or "was":

a. If I _____ in the USA, I would have tried to learn as much English as possible. **b.** If he _____ really interested in his job, he would do his work more carefully. **c.** Before they came to Germany, they _____ in England for some time. **d.** If I _____ there last week, I would certainly have helped you. **e.** If I had known that he _____ in Birmingham, I would have sent him the leaflets. **f.** What would you have done if you _____ here? – I would have talked to the chief engineer first, I think.

21

9 CB radios: Accessories and specifications

1. Please use the following words and figures to complete the texts below and on the following page ("Accessories" and "Specifications"):

Accessories

> convenient, extra, great, integrated, noisy (2×), regular, right, 0.7, 2¼, 3, 5.5, 23, 800

ACCESSORIES. Mobile power microphone. Not much larger than a _____ microphone, plugs _____ into your mobile unit. You can get the _____ modulation you sometimes need.

Telephone handset. Just like your home telephone, except for the _____ push-to-talk button. _____ for use in _____ vehicles. Complete with coiled cord and five-pin DIN plug.

⋕⋕⋕hy-range I

SPECIFICATIONS

General
Channels: _____ crystal-controlled channels
Size: width: 7 in; depth: 7½ in; height: _____ in
Shipping weight: _____ lbs

Receiver
Output: 2 watts
Sensitivity: _____ μV

Transmitter
Modulation: AM
Input: 5 watts
Output: more than _____ watts

9

Desk power microphone. This desk unit has an _____ preamplifier. _____ ohm impedance, five-pin DIN plug, coiled cord.
Power speaker. A high-quality, amplified speaker, most useful in _____, mobile areas (often used in trucks, for instance). Large amplifier produces 3 watts. 6' cord and plug supplied.

> **New words and phrases:**
> **convenient** [kən'viːnjənt] bequem; passend; angenehm
> **impedance** ['impədəns] Impedanz, Scheinwiderstand
> **handset** Telefonhörer
> **push-to-talk button** *(etwa:)* Sprechknopf
> **five-pin DIN plug** fünfpoliger DIN-Stecker
> **desk** [desk] Schreibtisch
> **desk microphone** Tischmikrofon
> **preamplifier** Vorverstärker
> **speaker** = loudspeaker
> **ship** versenden; (aus)liefern
> **shipping weight** Versandgewicht
> **receiver** *(hier:)* Empfänger, Empfangsteil
> **sensitivity** [sensi'tiviti] Empfindlichkeit
> **output** Ausgangsleistung
> **input** ['input] Leistungsaufnahme

2 Please complete the following sentences:

a. If you want to find a good restaurant, you must look _____ _____ CB antennas _____ the parking lot. **b.** Your FCC license is good _____ five years. **c.** In talking _____ the radio, truckers often use slang expressions. **d.** "You can generally tell the good restaurants _____ the number of CB antennas _____ the cars on the parking lot," said the trucker. **e.** "Smokey with ears" is a slang expression _____ "police with CB radios".

3 Please put in "who" or "whose":

a. The trucker _____ vehicle you can see over there has just had an accident on the highway. **b.** The policeman _____ was monitoring Channel 9 drove to the location and caught the hit-and-run driver. **c.** The man _____ CB radio I'm repairing lives in Pasadena. **d.** The reporter _____ car was stopped by a policeman spends a lot of time on the highways. **e.** The man _____ was asked about CB radios has a radio store in Houston, Texas. **f.** Travelling by hovercraft is a good thing for people _____ get seasick very easily. **g.** Mr Lawrence, _____ was the chairman of the meeting, asked him about his opinion.

10 APU

1 Please read this text ...

The APU makes the A300B completely independent of ground power sources. It can be used for all the major services:

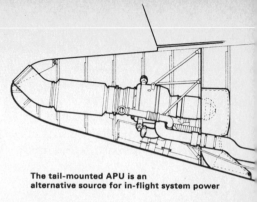

The tail-mounted APU is an alternative source for in-flight system power

- Air conditioning of passenger and flight compartments on the ground and in flight up to an altitude of 15,000 ft (4600 m).

- Electric power – 60 or 90 kVA nominal rating up to 30,000 ft (9100 m). The generator and control unit are identical to those on the main engines.

- Hydraulic power via two electric pumps.

- Engine starting.

APU starting is fully automatic, power being supplied by the main batteries. It may also be started from a main engine generator or from a ground power source.

... and find the word in the text that belongs to each explanation:

a. <u>altitude</u>   height above the earth's surface
b. _____ a means of making the air pure and of controlling its temperature and humidity in a room, building, etc.
c. _____ machine that produces electricity when driven by an engine or a water wheel
d. _____ machine for moving liquids or gases by pressure or suction
e. _____ a person who is carried in a car, bus, airplane, etc.
f. _____ having to do with water or other liquids in motion; operated by the pressure of a liquid or by the force of liquid in motion

2 Please make sentences according to the example:

trucker / see / last / Thursday / interested in CB radios
The trucker I saw last Thursday is interested in CB radios.

a. engineer / show the machine to / last Tuesday / very efficient **b.** operator / talk to / yesterday / from Birmingham **c.** man / meet / in Pasadena / policeman **d.** driver / tell about the restaurant / yesterday / still in London **e.** woman / tell you about / this morning / student

New words and phrases:

nominal rating ['nɔminəl] Nennleistung
identical [ai'dentikəl] identisch; (genau) gleich
via ['vaiə] über; via
pure ['pjuə] rein; sauber; pur
humidity [hju:'miditi] Feuchtigkeit; Feuchtigkeitsgehalt
... **power being supplied by the main batteries**... wobei die Energie von den Hauptbatterien kommt
undercarriage ['ʌndəkæridʒ] Fahrgestell

3 Please put in "who(m)" where necessary:

a. Mr Mills, _____ lived in Texas for some years, likes American cars very much. **b.** Mr Baldinger, _____ the company's German representative, would like to have some leaflets in German. **c.** Do you know the man _____ repaired the milling machine? **d.** Mr Eaton, _____ is one of our chief engineers, spent two months in the USA last year. **e.** This is the man _____ I talked to in the workshop.

4 Please complete:

a. The Rolls-Royce engine has a thrust of about 50,000 _____. **b.** The APU can be operated _____ the ground.

"Don't you ever ask me to check your undercarriage again!" ▷

11 A crossword puzzle

1 Try to solve the following crossword puzzle. Most of the words you need are connected with cars:

Across: **1** rapid motion back and forth; **4** vehicle; **8** abbreviation for "company"; **9** reddish-brown coating that forms on iron or steel when exposed to air; **11** English name for "Wankel" engine: _____ engine; **13** abbreviation for "manganese"; **14** devices for controlling the flow of a fluid; **16** abbreviation for "kilometre"; **17** abbreviation for "hectare"; **22** increase in speed

Down: **2** large vehicle that carries a lot of people; **3** circular, air-filled rubber tubes around the rims of wheels; **5** abbreviation for "alternating current"; **6** sign for controlling road traffic; **7** abbreviation for "hour"; **9** public way for vehicles; **10** large container for holding a liquid; **12** abbreviation for "American Standards Association"; **14** abbreviation for "volt-amperes"; **15** abbreviation for "pound" (= weight); **18** English automobile club (abbreviation); **19** abbreviation for "aluminium"; **20** abbreviation for "pascal"; **21** abbreviation for "silicon"

2 Please translate the following sentences into English:

New words and phrases:

back and forth [fɔːθ] hin und her
reddish-brown ['rediʃ-'braun] rotbraun
coating Überzug; Belag
increase Steigerung; Vergrößerung
circular rund; kreisförmig
rim [rim] Felge; Kranz
public way öffentlicher Weg

a. Ich habe ihm gestern gesagt, daß er die Maschine so schnell wie möglich reparieren muß. b. Wann wollen Sie die Klimaanlage einbauen? – Wahrscheinlich nächste Woche. c. Sie hätten ihm sagen sollen, daß er für dieses Experiment eine Papierscheibe braucht. d. Sie sollten den Wagen waschen lassen, wenn Sie in der Werkstatt sind. e. Hat er Ihnen gesagt, daß wir einen neuen Computer bekommen? – Ja, ich habe gestern mit ihm gesprochen. f. Wenn ich gewußt hätte, daß der Wagen einen so hohen Benzinverbrauch hat, hätte ich ihn sicher nicht gekauft. g. Sie brauchen den Brief nicht übersetzen zu lassen. h. Sie hätten zuerst die Bedienungsanleitung lesen sollen.

3 Please put in "as", "but", "so" or "than":

a. There's room enough in the front _____ not _____ much space in the back. b. I'm not sure whether the new Jaguar has the beauty of the old E-type, _____ the new car looks quite a lot heavier. c. The vibration stopped _____ the speed increased. d. The new Jaguar costs more _____ nine thousand pounds.

"Go home? You're asking me to go to a place where ninety per cent of all accidents occur?" ▷

12 Electric arc furnaces

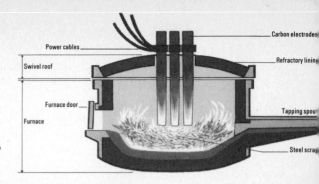

1 Please put in "the" where necessary:

a. Unlike _____ open-hearth process, _____ electric arc process uses only _____ cold scrap metal.
Today, _____ electric arc process is often used for making large tonnages of _____ widely used steels.

b. At _____ start of the process, the electrodes are withdrawn and _____ roof swung clear. The steel scrap is then charged into _____ furnace.

c. When charging is complete, the roof is swung back into position and _____ electrodes lowered into the furnace. A powerful electric current is passed through _____ charge, an arc is struck, and the heat generated melts the scrap.

d. _____ lime, fluorspar and iron oxide are added, and these combine with impurities to form liquid slag.

e. From time to _____ time, samples are taken and analysed.

f. Then, the slag containing _____ impurities is taken off _____ molten metal.

g. The furnace is then tilted and _____ steel is tapped from the furnace into a teeming ladle suspended from an overhead crane.

CHARGING SCRAP

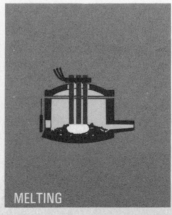
MELTING

ADDITIONS

2 Please put in "kind" or "way":

a. An American company has developed a new _____ of material that can be used for very high temperatures. **b.** We'll have to find a more efficient _____ to coat the metal surfaces. **c.** Some loudspeakers have a two-_____ system. **d.** He lost the rivets on his _____ to the workshop.

3 Please complete:

a. Can you show me the list you drew _____? – Yes, certainly. **b.** The new pipe insulation system is very easy to use: You just snap the sections _____. **c.** It took me more than six hours to put the kit _____. **d.** I don't know what these appliances are used _____. **e.** She didn't tell me what she is worried _____. **f.** I forgot the name of the man I talked _____ when I was in London. **g.** The accumulator must not be left _____ for more than five seconds at a time.

New words and phrases:

unlike im Gegensatz zu; anders als
tonnage ['tʌnidʒ] Produktionsmenge; Tonnage
widely used steels vielgebrauchte Stahlsorten
swing clear wegschwenken
charge beschicken
swing back zurückschwenken
... is passed through the charge ... wird durch die Charge geleitet
lime [laim] Kalk
fluorspar ['fluəspɑː] Flußspat
iron oxide ['ɔksaid] Eisenoxid
impurities [im'pjuəritiz] Verunreinigungen
analyse ['ænəlaiz] analysieren; untersuchen
take off the molten metal vom flüssigen Metall entfernen
tap [tæp] *(Schlacke:)* abziehen; *(Metall:)* abstechen
teeming ladle ['tiːmiŋ] Gießpfanne
overhead Frei-; Hoch-; obenliegend
overhead crane Hallenkran

12

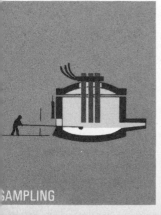
SAMPLING

SLAGGING

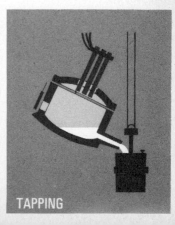
TAPPING

13 The bridge is breaking up!

1 Please connect the sentences below by using "although", "but", "when" or "while":

a. they had made their calculations very carefully two sections of the metal span did not fit
b. Mr Hindshaw was talking to his men the buckled section changed colour
c. the buckled section changed colour from rust to blue-grey Mr Hindshaw knew that the span was taking too great a strain
d. Jack Hindshaw arrived on the scene it was already too late
e. Jack Hindshaw called his men to the lift again he was too late

2 Please find the correct explanation for the words on the left:

collapse	**a.** be afraid of
crash	**c.** be right in size and shape
fear	**d.** change to a liquid by heating
fit	**e.** fall down; fall in
hoist	**f.** fall suddenly and noisily
join	**g.** lift up; raise
melt	**h.** put together
remove	**i.** provide
span	**j.** reach or extend over
supply	**k.** shake
tremble	**l** take away

3 Please put in "at", "down", "for", "in", "into", "on" or "to":

New words and phrases:
fall in einstürzen; einfallen
lift up hochheben
extend (over) [iks'tend] sich erstrecken (über)
abroad [ə'brɔːd] im Ausland; ins Ausland
pleasure ['pleʒə] Vergnügen; Spaß; Freude
ratio ['reiʃiəu] Verhältnis; Quotient
a big factor ein wichtiger Faktor
mpg = miles per gallon
chauffeur ['ʃəufə] Fahrer; Chauffeur

a. Has she gone abroad _____ pleasure or on business? – On business, I think. **b.** A massive tower was to be built _____ each end of the bridge. **c.** The Australian managers did not believe _____ the box girder system that was _____ be used _____ the bridge. **d.** After a while, they found that two sections of the metal span (prefabricated _____ the ground) did not fit. **e.** It was decided _____ weight the sections with 80 tons of concrete blocks to bring it _____. **f.** When Jack Hindshaw arrived _____ the scene, he wondered whether he should take the men off the bridge. **g.** Then, with a sound like machine-gun fire, the bolts burst off _____ all directions and the whole, 2,000-ton section of the bridge collapsed. **h.** Nick Grosso, a welder, was _____ the span when it crashed _____ the river 155 ft below. **i.** "It was awful," he said. "I went _____ with the span. When I woke up, I was _____ the ground."

"Weight ratio's a big factor in mpg, sir. If I were you I'd get a smaller chauffeur!"

14 Mathematics for fun (I)

1 Please try to solve this "mathematical" problem:

> You are driving to the airport, which is ten miles away. You must drive at an average speed of 60 miles per hour if you want to catch your plane.
>
> On the way to the airport, you run into very heavy traffic. Therefore, your average speed is down to 30 miles per hour for the first five miles.
>
> What must the average speed be for the rest of the way to the airport if you want to be on time for your plane?
>
> *(Solution see key to the exercises)*

2 Please use one part from "A" and one part from "B" to form complete sentences:

A 1 Although Ms Brown had never been to England or the USA,
   2 Everybody was listening carefully
   3 Since this gas is highly explosive,
   4 When he saw black petrol fumes come out of the exhaust,
   5 When they saw they could not find the cause of the trouble,
   6 If he had told me that the spaceship was controlled by a computer,

B 1 he knew there was something seriously wrong with the engine.
   2 I wouldn't have bought a ticket for the flight.
   3 she did some very good translations for our company.
   4 they asked Mr Eaton, who was well-known as an excellent troubleshooter, to have a look at the electronic equipment.
   5 when the announcement came over the loudspeaker.
   6 you should always keep it away from fire.

14

3 Please complete:

a. "What _____ 'FM' stand for?" – "'Frequency modulation', I think."
b. They _____ use plastics for these components if they knew how much money they could save.
c. You should have explained the machine _____ him.

4 Please choose the correct form:

a. She told me she didn't mind *(travel/travelling)* in a computer-controlled spacecraft.
b. What am I supposed *(to say/saying)* when he asks me about his car? – Well, tell him it will be repaired as soon as possible.
c. Do you *(mind/minding)* if I use your tools for an hour or so? – No, not at all.

5 Please put in "in" or "on":

a. He came home very late _____ the evening.
b. _____ the morning of October 15, they began to straighten out the buckle _____ the steel spans.
c. The Australian managers did not believe _____ the box girder system that was to be used for the bridge.

New words and phrases:

mathematics [mæθəˈmætiks] Mathematik
away [əˈwei] weg; fort
ten miles away zehn Meilen entfernt
catch a plane ein Flugzeug erreichen
run into heavy traffic in starken Verkehr geraten
on time pünktlich
Ms [miz] (Ms Brown = Frau Brown: "Ms" ist eine moderne Anredeform, die sich aus "Miss" und "Mrs" zusammensetzt
explosive [iksˈpləusiv] explosiv
fumes [fju:mz] Dämpfe; Qualm; Rauch
troubleshooter [ˈtrʌblʃu:tə] (= qualifizierter Mitarbeiter, der immer dann gerufen wird, wenn es Schwierigkeiten oder Störungen gibt)
you must keep it away from fire Sie müssen es vom Feuer fernhalten
stand [stænd] (stood [stud] – have stood) stehen

15 Computer games

1 Please do the following "computer games":

> **Necessary equipment:** 1 pocket calculator
>
> Pick a three-digit number in which all the digits are the same (e. g. 333, 444, 666, etc.).
>
> Punch the sum of the digits on the pocket calculator, then multiply by 37 – and the original number will come up again.

> **Necessary equipment:** 1 pocket calculator
>
> There are 142 engineers and 154 technicians working on the country's 69 oilfields for five years. What's the name of the company they are working for?
>
> Punch the first eight figures (= 14 215 469) on your pocket calculator, then multiply by five. The answer, of course, is 71 077 345.
>
> Now turn the pocket calculator around (rotate it 180 degrees) and you can see the name of the company the engineers and technicians are working for.
>
> *(Solution see key to the exercises)*

2 Please complete:

a. The Speech-Plus calculator understands a spoken vocabulary _____ 24 words. b. You don't have _____ look _____ the visual display _____ determine if an entry is correct. c. The calculator has a rechargeable battery and is small enough _____ fit _____ your pocket. d. Apart _____ that, it also has a button _____ turning the speaker _____ or _____ and _____ volume control. e. The price includes a shockproof case _____ speaker.

3 Please make sentences according to the example:

> chief engineer / angry / mistakes
> Not only the chief engineer is angry about the mistakes.

a. manager / interested / new computers **b.** politicians / worried / future **c.** Joan / afraid / get seasick **d.** technicians / looking forward / holidays **e.** Jack / trying to get admitted / college

4 Please use "mind" when you translate the following sentences:

a. Ich habe nichts dagegen, wenn er nach England fährt. **b.** Warum haben Sie es sich anders überlegt? – Nun, ich finde die neue Lösung besser. **c.** Sie hat sich entschlossen, die Stellung in den USA anzunehmen. **d.** Haben Sie etwas dagegen, wenn ich den Computer benutze? – Nein, ganz sicher nicht.

New words and phrases:

game [geim] Spiel
pocket ['pɔkit] Tasche (an Kleidungsstücken)
pocket calculator Taschenrechner
punch on your pocket calculator in den Taschenrechner eingeben
turn around herumdrehen
pick [pik] aussuchen; (aus)wählen; sich entscheiden für
digit ['didʒit] Ziffer (0 bis 9); Stelle (= Ziffer)
three-digit number dreistellige Zahl
... will come up again ... wird wieder auftauchen
turn off abschalten; ausschalten (Geräte etc.)
volume control Lautstärkeregler

---

5 Please put in "do" or "make":

a. Well, the computer doesn't work. What are we going to _____ now? – Use our heads, I would say. **b.** Aluminium? No, I don't think aluminium will _____. We'll have to use steel. **c.** The new models _____ more than 100 miles per hour. **d.** These electronic devices _____ it possible to run the machines automatically.

"We've been trying hard – that's the only answer we can get!" ▷

16 Briv – high-speed riveting

1 Please put in the words and find out which explanation (a, b, c or d) belongs to which diagram (in the correct sequence):

action, component, head, hole, machine, mandrel, rivet, steel, tail

a. The _____ continues to be pulled through the rivet, expanding the rivet shank to fill the hole. This _____ continues until the material is clamped tight.

b. When the _____ is finally installed in the hole, the hardened _____ mandrel is withdrawn.

c. After the hole has been drilled into the _____, the magazine-loaded rivet is placed into the _____.

d. When the riveting _____ is operated, the hardened steel mandrel is drawn from the _____ end of the rivet, compressing the rivet material towards its _____.

2 Please choose the correct form of the words in brackets (-ly?):

a. *(Blind)* rivets are *(usual)* used in joints that can be reached from only one side. **b.** Magazine loading results in a *(real)* *(efficient)* fastening at low cost. **c.** However, *(apart)* from their *(main)* use in blind applications, blind rivets are being *(increasing)* used in joints where both sides can be reached. **d.** It has been found that they can *(usual)* simplify assembly, save *(considerable)* amounts of metal, and decrease cost. **e.** Moreover, blind riveting can be brought to the work – an *(especial)* *(valuable)* advantage where large assemblies are involved.

3 Please put in "no", "none" or "not":

a. We asked them to attend the meeting last Wednesday but _____ of them came. **b.** An aluminium window means _____ more corrosion and _____ more maintenance. **c.** Will we need a new shaft for the engine? – I hope _____. **d.** Is he interested in going to England next year? – _____, _____ at all. **e.** I wanted some screws for the shelf but there were _____ in the workshop. **f.** I think we will have to ask Mr Jasper, our troubleshooter, to have a look at the engine. I'm sure _____ other man can repair it. **g.** I'm afraid _____ of the engineers will be able to attend the meeting next Monday afternoon.

> **New words and phrases:**
>
> **sequence** ['siːkwəns] Reihenfolge; (Aufeinander)Folge; Reihe
> **clamp** [klæmp] festklemmen; befestigen
> **clamped tight** straff festgeklemmt
> **blind rivets** Blindnieten
> **increasingly** immer mehr
> **simplify** ['simplifai] vereinfachen
> **... can be brought to work** ... kann an den Arbeitsplatz gebracht werden
> **where large assemblies are involved** wo man es mit großen Montagearbeiten zu tun hat
> **it dates from ...** es stammt aus dem Jahre ...

16

"It is believed to be one of the finest and largest in England – one hundred and thirty feet high, with a capacity of eight million cubic feet. It dates from nineteen hundred and ten, and took two years to build. There are over nineteen thousand rivets, and ...

17 Mathematics for fun (II)

1 Please try to solve this "mathematical" problem:

> Imagine a train that is a mile long. This train is approaching a mile-long tunnel at a speed of 60 miles per hour. How long will it take for the train to get through the tunnel?
>
> *(Solution see key to the exercises)*

2 Please choose the correct explanation for the words on the left:

aerosol	**a.** accurately turned rod, over which metal is forged, drawn or shaped during working
bumper	
crucible	**b.** container of substance packed under pressure with a device for releasing it as fine spray
die	**c.** heat-resistant vessel in which metals are melted
foundry	**d.** in the wheels of a vehicle, that part of the tire in contact with the road or rail
mandrel	
tread	**e.** metal bar attached to front and back of motor vehicles to reduce damage in collision
	f. metal block used in stamping operations; it is pressed down on to the metal sheet, on which the pattern of the block's surface is reproduced
	g. workshop in which metal objects are made by casting in moulds

3 Please put in the question tags:

a. The young recruit was color-blind, _____? **b.** The green button alerts the president, _____? **c.** The senior officer didn't want to be interrupted, _____? **d.** He should have allowed the recruit to answer, _____?

4 Please complete:

a. A radial steel tire _____ seals itself when punctured by nails has been developed by an American company. **b.** These buttons can destroy the world, young man. If you press the wrong _____, you'll start the Third World War. **c.** Now please be quiet, _____ you. **d.** That red button over there, well, that's the most important _____.

5 Please put in "the" where necessary:

a. You'll be in _____ charge of the control room. **b.** There is virtually no loss of _____ air. **c.** The tire contains a liner system of _____ modified sponge rubber. **d.** The recruit is listening to _____ officer. **e.** The hole will be sealed, even if the puncturing object is not kept in _____ tread.

New words and phrases:

tunnel ['tʌnl] Tunnel
aerosol ['ɛərəsɔl] Sprühdose, Spraydose
die [dai] Gesenk; Form, Preßform
accurately turned ['ækjuritli] präzise gedreht
rod [rɔd] Stab; Stange
forge [fɔːdʒ] schmieden
shape formen; umformen
substance ['sʌbstəns] Substanz; Stoff
pack [pæk] (ver)packen
release [ri'liːs] ablassen; freigeben
spray [sprei] Sprühnebel
contact ['kɔntækt] Kontakt; Berührung; Verbindung
stamp [stæmp] pressen
reproduce [riːprə'djuːs] nachbilden; reproduzieren
cast [kɑːst] (cast – have cast) gießen
mould (*US auch:* mold) [məuld] Gußform

18 BD-5J specifications

1 Please put the figures on the right into the text on the left:

Performance	
Maximum speed: 276 mph at sea level, _____ mph at an altitude of _____ ft	10,000
	585
	17
Range at 10,000 ft altitude: _____ miles with a 20-minute reserve	960
	6
Take-off distance: _____ ft	450
Landing distance: 1,000 ft ground roll	12.4
	1,800
	55
Dimensions	267

Wing span: _____ ft   Empty weight: _____ lbs
Length: _____ ft   Gross weight: _____ lbs
Height: _____ ft   Useful load: 510 lbs
Fuel capacity: _____ gal

2 Please put in "very" or "very much":

a. After working in the factory for more than ten hours, they were _____ tired. **b.** He's not _____ interested in making money. **c.** She loves her old car _____. **d.** He speaks English _____ well.

3 Please put in "even", "ever" or "every":

a. They checked _____ part of the machine, _____ the nuts and bolts. **b.** Have you _____ been to Birmingham? – No, I haven't. **c.** That's the sexiest plane I've _____ seen! **d.** In the future, _____ buses will be computer-controlled.

4 What do these expressions mean? Please find the correct explanation and mark it with a cross:

New words and phrases:

sea level Meeresspiegel
range Reichweite
reserve [ri'zə:v] Reserve
take-off distance Startstrecke
landing distance Landestrecke
ground roll Landelauf (= Strecke, auf der das Flugzeug bei der Landung Bodenkontakt hat)
wing span Flügelspannweite
useful load Zuladung
cross [krɔs] Kreuz
nothing but trouble nichts als Ärger

to a small extent – ☐ **a.** only for small components ☐ **b.** in one direction only ☐ **c.** not very much
off the main road – ☐ **a.** near the main road ☐ **b.** along the main road
take them away – ☐ **a.** remove them ☐ **b.** change them
it's far from easy – ☐ **a.** it's very easy ☐ **b.** it isn't easy at all
get admitted to college – ☐ **a.** fail the college examination ☐ **b.** find a place in college
nothing but trouble – ☐ **a.** not much trouble ☐ **b.** more trouble than before ☐ **c.** a lot of trouble
he failed to understand – ☐ **a.** he understood, but very slowly ☐ **b.** he didn't understand
who is in charge? – ☐ **a.** who has to pay for it? ☐ **b.** who has the responsibility?
it's virtually maintenance-free – ☐ **a.** it needs hardly any maintenance ☐ **b.** it doesn't need any maintenance at all

5 Please translate the following sentences:

a. Warum sind Sie vorige Woche nicht nach England gefahren? – Ich mußte zuerst die neuen Computerprogramme schreiben. **b.** Wenn Sie den BD-5J-Jet zusammenbauen wollen, brauchen Sie einige Werkzeugmaschinen. **c.** Einige Leute warten schon seit Wochen auf die Genehmigung der Federal Aviation Agency. **d.** Der neue Taschenrechner hat ein eingebautes Vokabular von 24 Wörtern. **e.** Wenn Sie den Chefingenieur gefragt hätten, wären diese Schwierigkeiten nicht aufgetaucht. **f.** Es gibt nicht viele Nietmaschinen, die eine so hohe Leistung haben. **g.** Sind Sie schon mal in New Mexico gewesen? – Ja, ich habe vor zwei Jahren meinen Urlaub dort verbracht.

19 The pleasure of driving

1 Please complete the text below by putting in the following words:

> easy, few, grey, head-on, interesting, little, often, painted, possible, practical, right, serious, several, very

More fun for motorists?

a. Was the American journalist _____ when he suggested painting pictures on the concrete walls that _____ divide the lanes of American freeways?

b. These concrete walls have a _____ purpose, of course: the prevention of _____ collisions. But there is no reason, the journalist wrote, why they have to be so _____ and uninteresting.

c. It is true that painting the freeway concrete walls would not be _____ since they are _____ miles long and only a _____ feet high. But some objects, he suggested, could _____ well be painted on the walls. A mile or two of _____ grass, for instance, would give the motorists a taste of the country before they leave the city. Or perhaps a boa constrictor. It is just the _____ shape for freeway concrete walls.

d. And if the boa constrictor was painted in colours that glow in the dark ... well, that would look quite _____, wouldn't it. The journalist thought it might also be _____ to paint pretty girls on the concrete walls. There would, however, be some difficulties since many drivers would then pay _____ attention to the road and the traffic. Seeing a boa constrictor, however, would sober up a drunken driver faster than anything else.

2 Please answer:

> Why didn't you check the battery? (necessary tools) – Well, we would have checked it if we had had the necessary tools.

a. Why didn't you use the computer? (know how to program it) **b.** Why didn't you carry out the experiment? (some fuse wire) **c.** Why didn't you repair the riveting machine? (new mandrel) **d.** Why didn't you buy the Speech-Plus pocket calculator? (enough money) **e.** Why didn't you assemble the plane yourself? (some machine tools)

3 Please put in "so" or "such":

a. Several companies are working together now to find out whether _____ a system can be built. **b.** If the answer is yes, ALI could be ready within the next six years or _____. **c.** Why didn't you call Mr Brown? He's _____ a good troubleshooter. **d.** Will we have to buy a new shaft for the engine? – No, I don't think _____. **e.** I don't know where he lives, _____ I couldn't ask him to come to the brain-storming session on Wednesday.

4 Which of the two words in the brackets is the correct one?

a. Tidal power stations use the tides *(as/for)* a source of energy. **b.** The *(only/single)* tidal power station that has gone *(into/to)* full operation is in France. **c.** ALI consists *(in/of)* a series of inductive loops *(connected/set)* into the road surface. **d.** *(All the/The whole)* loops are linked *(at/to)* computers which can sense where the car wants to go.

New words and phrases:

journalist ['dʒɜːnəlist] Journalist
freeway *(US)* Autobahn
prevention [pri'venʃən] Verhütung; Verhinderung
head-on collision Frontalzusammenstoß
uninteresting ['ʌn'intrəstiŋ] uninteressant
grass [grɑːs] Gras
a taste of the country [teist] einen Vorgeschmack auf das Land (= im Gegensatz zu Stadt)
boa constrictor ['bəuə kən'striktə] (= Riesenschlange)
glow [gləu] leuchten; glühen
in the dark in der Dunkelheit
girl [gɜːl] Mädchen
pay attention to something [ə'tenʃən] einer Sache Aufmerksamkeit widmen
sober ['səubə] nüchtern
sober up nüchtern machen
a drunken driver ['drʌŋkən] ein betrunkener Fahrer

19

20 Qualified draughtsmen wanted

1 Please complete the advertisement shown below ("Draughtsmen") by putting in "for", "in", "of", "to" or "with":

Draughtsmen

We are seeking qualified draughtsmen ___ a number ___ years experience ___ the field ___ steam generation plant ___ ships.

You will be involved ___ the preparation ___ drawings ___ our own works and ___ subsidiaries throughout Europe and ___ the USA.

We can offer plenty ___ variety ___ this specialized field, ___ excellent prospects ___ promotion and a good salary. Our benefits package includes profit share, free lunches, and generous holidays. Assistance ___ accommodation can also be arranged.

___ further information, including details ___ salary and benefits, please write ___:

John Richmond, Personnel Manager
Brooke & Russell Boilers Ltd
Kennington Works
Manchester M12 5JL

Telephone: 061-4715892

44

2 Please put in "each" or "every":

a. Do you know Mr Richmond? – Oh yes, I do. In fact, we see _____ other nearly _____ day when we have lunch. **b.** How much are these books here? – Two pounds _____. **c.** The buses to Kennington run _____ fifteen minutes. **d.** When the ALI system is introduced, _____ motorist will have to buy an additional electronic unit for his car. **e.** The Briv riveting machine is available in three diameters with four grip lengths in _____ diameter. **f.** This new electric cooker has five heat settings. Push-button units and controls give you an exact heat for _____ setting.

New words and phrases:

preparation [prepəˈreiʃən] Herstellung; Vorbereitung; Aufbereitung
works Werk, Betrieb
subsidiaries [səbˈsidjəriz] Tochtergesellschaften
variety *(hier:)* Abwechslung
specialised [ˈspeʃəlaizd] spezializiert
promotion [prəˈmouʃən] Beförderung
package [ˈpækidʒ] Paket
share [ʃɛə] Beteiligung; Anteil; sich beteiligen
lunch [lʌntʃ] Mittagessen
boiler [ˈbɔilə] Kessel
we see each other wir sehen uns
book [buk] Buch
two pounds each zwei Pfund das Stück (pro Stück)
ill [il] krank
out of order nicht in Ordnung; kaputt

3 Please answer:

Why didn't you get the walls painted? (have enough tools)
Well, I would have got them painted if I'd had enough tools.

Why didn't you get the drawing finished? (draughtsman is ill)
Well, I would have got it finished if the draughtsman hadn't been ill.

a. Why didn't you get the engine tuned? (have enough time to go to the workshop) **b.** Why didn't you get the air purifier installed? (technician is on holiday) **c.** Why didn't you get the letter translated? (have someone who can translate letters into English) **d.** Why didn't you get the electronic equipment checked? (have a good technician) **e.** Why didn't you get the jet assembled? (machine tools are out of order) **f.** Why didn't you get the electrodes replaced? (have new ones) **g.** Why didn't you get the car washed? (garage is closed) **h.** Why didn't you get the riveting machine repaired? (have the necessary spare parts)

21 Fiesta facts and figures

1 Please complete:

a. Ford _____ about two billion German marks in the Fiesta. **b.** Above _____, they said, the car must be easy to repair. **c.** Over 27 per cent of small-car owners gave low price _____ the main reason for buying the car, but 43 per cent said they bought the car because of the low running _____, too. **d.** The rear braking system is adjusted automatically _____ soon _____ there is any wear. **e.** Transmission and clutch can _____ removed _____ taking out the engine. **f.** The company claim the servicing costs will _____ at least 22 per cent _____ than with any other car in the same class.

The new wedge combustion chamber gives a good combination of performance, low fuel consumption and minimum exhaust emission.

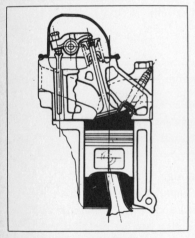

Inspection hole and simple tool allow an easy check on brake pad wear.

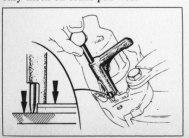

ENGINE (_____ cc)
Bore . . . . . . _____ mm
Stroke . . . . . _____ mm
Compression ratio _____ : 1
Maximum power
(DIN) . . . . 40 PS
Maximum torque at
_____ rpm . . . . 64 Nm

BRAKES

Type . . . Diagonally-split
        hydraulic circuits
Front . . . . Discs
Rear . . . . Drums

STEERING

Type . . . Rack and pinion
Ratio . . . . . . _____ to 1
Number of turns 3.4
Turning circle . . . _____ m

2 Please put the figures below into the text on the left:

8.3
55.7
9.3
957
18.62
74
2,700

3 Please put in "fine", "good" or "well":

a. The report said that the pedals were small but _____ spaced. b. The opportunities that exist in our company are very _____ indeed. c. The substance that is packed under pressure in an aerosol is released as a _____ spray. d. How is Mr Richmond? – Very _____, thank you. e. Truckers usually know all the _____ restaurants along the highways. f. That is a very _____-designed bridge, I must say. g. Mr Baldinger speaks English very _____. h. We had some trouble at the new plant last week but now everything seems to be going _____. i. The valves they sent us yesterday are not very _____. j. I'm afraid he didn't do his job very _____.

New words and phrases:

running costs laufende Kosten
wear Abnutzung
bore [bɔː, bɔə] Bohrung
stroke Hub
compression ratio ['reiʃiəu] Verdichtungsverhältnis
torque [tɔːk] Drehmoment
diagonal [dai'ægənəl] diagonal
split [split] geteilt
rack and pinion ['ræk ən 'pinjən] Zahnstangenturns Umdrehungen
turning circle Wendekreis
combustion [kəm'bʌstʃən] Verbrennung
wedge combustion chamber keilförmiger Brennraum
combination [kɔmbi'neiʃən] Kombination; Verbindung
exhaust emission [i'miʃən] Schadstoffemission (= Ausstoß)
inspection [in'spekʃən] Inspektion; Prüfung
inspection hole Schauloch
brake pad [pæd] Bremsbelag

21

47

22 NASA facilities: Solar heating and cooling systems

1. Please read the text below and answer the questions on the opposite page ("Right or Wrong?"):

The NASA picture on the right shows a remote weather station in California, powered by solar cells which are covered with plastic as a protection against the weather. – At the bottom, you can see a NASA test facility for solar heating and cooling at the Marshall Space Flight Center in Huntsville, Alabama. The solar panels are arranged in such a way that they receive the maximum amount of sunlight: They are mounted on the south side of an angled roof (45 degrees). The sun heats the water circulating through the solar panels, and the heated water – stored in a 4,500 gallon insulated tank – is used to operate an air-conditioning unit in summer or to heat air in winter.

So far, the solar panels have worked as expected with no problems. The air conditioner, after extensive testing, is at present being modified to operate at greatly increased efficiency at a lower water temperature than originally planned.

Data from the instruments indicates a daily energy collection of up to half a million BTU.

2 Right or wrong ("R" or "W"):

	R	W
a. The weather station in California is covered with plastic.	☐	☐
b. The roof is angled so that it receives the maximum amount of sunlight.	☐	☐
c. The sun heats the water in a 4,500 gallon tank.	☐	☐
d. There have been no problems with the test facility in Huntsville, Alabama.	☐	☐
e. The air-conditioning unit is only used in summer.	☐	☐
f. The solar panels have been modified to work more efficiently at lower water temperatures.	☐	☐
g. The test facility in Alabama is in an industrial area.	☐	☐

New words and phrases:

south [sauθ] Süd-; Süden
summer ['sʌmə] Sommer
extensive [iks'tensiv] ausgedehnt
greatly sehr; außerordentlich; höchst
BTU (= British thermal ['θə:məl] unit; thermal = Wärme-) (1 BTU = 1055 J)
residential [rezi'denʃəl] Wohn- (= für Wohnzwecke)
industrial [in'dʌstriəl] Industrie-; industriell
pool [pu:l] Interessengemeinschaft; Ring; gemeinsamer Fond; *(Geld etc.:)* zusammenlegen; *(Kräfte etc.:)* vereinigen
working pool Arbeitsgemeinschaft
schedule [Br.: 'ʃedju:l; US: 'skedʒu:l] Liste; Tabelle
on schedule pünktlich; fahrplanmäßig
invoice ['invɔis] Rechnung

3 What do these expressions mean? Please find the correct explanation and mark it with a cross:

he's not likely to come – ☐   **a.** he will probably not come ☐   **b.** people don't want him to come ☐   **c.** he doesn't want to come

without extra charge – ☐   **a.** you won't get a separate invoice ☐   **b.** you don't have to pay more

they should pool their money – ☐   **a.** they ought to save their money ☐   **b.** they ought to invest their money ☐   **c.** they ought to put their money together

on schedule – ☐   **a.** as ordered ☐   **b.** in the list ☐   **c.** on time

you ought to make up your mind – ☐   **a.** you should reach a decision now ☐   **b.** you should think about it ☐   **c.** you shouldn't worry about it

23 Space age shooting gallery

1 Please use one part from "A" and one part from "B" to form complete sentences:

A 1 A minor disadvantage for training police is the fact
2 It's quite obvious that such an expensive shooting gallery
3 Instead of the chambers being bored completely through the cylinder
4 The fact that the laser beam shooting system can be installed in relatively small rooms
5 The TV pick-up system not only simulates the hits via a TV transmitter at the target,
6 Though the laser target looks very much like a normal target,

B 1 but scores each hit instantly and displays its precise value on a separate score board.
2 can only be bought by large organisations.
3 each is sealed at the front with a brass plug.
4 is a great advantage.
5 it's really a television pick-up system.
6 that there is no recoil as in a normal revolver.

2 Please put in "just" or "only":

a. The Japanese company that manufactures the laser beam shooting system hopes to sell it as a means of entertainment – _____ like bowling or miniature golf. **b.** I had _____ repaired the engine when it broke down again. **c.** The _____ thing you need for this experiment is a battery. **d.** The BD-5J weighs _____ about 500 pounds. **e.** The laser shooting gallery can be installed in small rooms, too. – Yes, but that's not the _____ advantage. **f.** This machine is _____ as good as the other. **g.** He arrived _____ as I was about to leave.

◁ *Inside the laser beam shooting gallery*

3 Which of the two words in brackets is the correct one?

New words and phrases:
minor ['mainə] geringfügig; unbedeutend
obvious ['ɔbviəs] offensichtlich
relative(ly) ['relətiv(li)] verhältnismäßig; relativ
simulate ['simjuleit] simulieren; vortäuschen
hit Treffer
via ['vaiə] über; mittels
score [skɔ:, skɔə] (Treffer, Tore, Punkte etc.:) aufzeichnen
instant(ly) ['instənt(li)] augenblicklich; unverzüglich
precise [pri'sais] präzise; genau
score board Anzeigetafel
plug Verschlußschraube; Pfropfen; Stöpsel
recoil [ri'kɔil, 'ri:kɔil] Rückstoß
I was about to leave ich wollte gerade gehen

23

a. Transistors are not *(easily/easy)* damaged but you'd better *(be/are)* *(careful/carefully)* with heat and excessive voltage. **b.** The nuts have a nylon patch *(added/adding)* to the *(threads/treads)* by spraying. **c.** Because temperatures often *(fall/go)* *(below/under)* freezing point in the winter, the solar panel system is filled *(by/with)* an anti-freeze solution. **d.** A laser amplifies radiation of frequencies within or near the *(distance/range)* of light.

4 Please make sentences:

repair / handgun – control console
Instead of repairing the handgun, she repaired the control console.

a. go / Birmingham – London **b.** write / letter – minutes **c.** say / "here you are" – "please" **d.** visit / foundry – car factory **e.** buy / an electric heater – a solar panel system **f.** use / steel for the machine parts – aluminium **g.** test / Fiesta – Jaguar XJ-S

5 Please complete:

a. I'd like to see what a laser beam shooting gallery looks like. – So _____ I. **b.** I won't sell their machines in Germany if they don't give me leaflets in German. – Neither _____ I. **c.** I've never tried to assemble an aircraft. – _____ have I. **d.** I can't imagine that anybody would spend so much money on a car. – Neither _____ I.
e. I don't understand how this shooting gallery works. – _____ do I.

24 From the compressor parts list

1 Please put in the correct illustration numbers:

Illus. No.	Description	Qty.	Part number
13	Brass pipe plug	1	1/2"
......	Breather tube with nuts	1	V 1544–44
5+6	Cap screw, socket head & washer	2	3V479–7
......	Crankcase	1	3F5671
......	Crankcase end cover (old style)	1	3H6314P1
......	Crankcase end cover gasket	1	3R8342
9	Flat steel washer	8	X1016T34
17	Flat steel washer	4	X1016T34
18	– Oil retainer	1	X1220T67
......	Hexagon head screw	8	3/8"-16 x 7/8"
......	Hexagon head screw	4	3/8"-16 x 7/8"
......	Nameplate with rivets	1	3W3936TP8
10	Oil gauge	1	3W21918
11	Oil gauge gasket	1	20A11CM212
7	Oil level shutdown switch	1	3R40619
4	Oil switch baffle	1	3R40725
......	Shaft end cover	1	3W21912P1
......	Shaft end cover gasket	1	3W21913
19	Tube connector	1	X1506-IC5

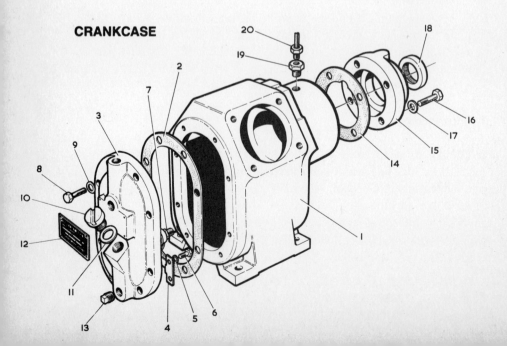

CRANKCASE

2 Please complete:

a. First you should fit _____ the circuit with a 2V accumulator. **b.** You can calculate the piston displacement – the volume of air swept _____ by the first stage piston – by using a formula. **c.** The investigations they carried _____ in an American car factory show that pneumatic tools can be more efficient. **d.** Which wire is the hotter when the current has been switched _____? – The thinner wire, of course. **e.** I don't know what the components for the new machine are made _____.

3 What do these abbreviations mean?

a. k = _____ **b.** N = _____
c. LCD = _____
d. VTOL = _____
e. J = _____ **f.** ppm = _____
g. R & D = _____ **h.** O. H. C. = _____ **i.** Cu = _____
j. C = _____ **k.** Fe = _____ **l.** Sb = _____
m. bhp = _____ **n.** Pa = _____ **o.** no = _____
p. STOL = _____ **q.** rad = _____
r. LED = _____
s. HD = _____
t. bbl = _____
u. deg = _____
v. rev/min = _____

New words and phrases:

Illus. = Illustration
Qty. = Quantity
parts list Teileliste
crankcase ['kræŋkeis] Kurbelgehäuse
end cover Endabdeckung
style [stail] Typ; Stil
baffle ['bæfl] Leitblech
cap screw Kopfschraube
socket head cap screw Innensechskantschraube
washer ['wɔʃə] Unterlegscheibe
shutdown Stillegung; Unterbrechung
shutdown switch Unterbrechungsschalter
hexagon head screw ['heksəgən] Sechskantschraube
retainer [ri'teinə] Dichtung(sring)
tube connector [kə'nektə] Rohrverbindungsstück
breather tube ['bri:ðə] Entlüfterrohr

Wukasch

25 Controlling cockroaches automatically

1 Please put in the following words:

> allow, connect, crawl, cut, install, last, power, unplug, use

a. Shock-M-All baseboards, produced by Shock-M-All Inc, Valley Stream, New York, _____ standard voltage to _____ a transformer placed high on the wall. **b.** The flame-retardant plastic covers _____ just enough space (0.25" or 6.35 mm) for an insect to _____ through but not for the fingers of a child. **c.** Shock-M-All baseboards are designed to _____ about twenty years with normal use and maintenance. **d.** Before removing the cover of the baseboard, please _____ the electric cord from the wall socket. **e.** The market for Shock-M-All baseboards is virtually unlimited: You can _____ them in every indoor place where insecticides are used. **f.** Shock-M-All baseboards will be available in two colours, in packages of 50 and 100, _____ in four-foot lengths. **g.** You can _____ the four-foot lengths with insulated connectors and cut them to any size if necessary.

2 Please make sentences:

> baseboards / clean – cover / lift
> Should the baseboards need to be cleaned, the cover can easily be lifted.

a. electronic equipment / repair – modules / replace   **b.** oil level / check – dipstick / insert   **c.** circulation pump / control – temperature switch / install   **d.** liquid / transport – pipe line / build

3 Please put in "it's" or "its":

a. The arcing current completed by _____ entry kills the cockroach.   **b.** _____ installed high on the wall where _____ out of reach.

4 Please complete:

a. The transformer _____ the wall induces a low, safe current. **b.** There is just enough space _____ an insect _____ crawl _____. **c.** The price depends _____ quantity and is exclusive _____ freight.

> **New words and phrases:**
>
> **gap** [gæp] Lücke; Spalt
> **affect** [əˈfekt] beeinflussen; angreifen
> **unaffected** unbeeinflußt
> **obtain** [əbˈtein] erlangen; erhalten; erreichen
> **ore** [ɔː, ɔə] Erz

5 Please find the correct explanations for the words on the right, and then put the words into the gaps in the sentences:

a. be undamaged or unaffected by something: *The plastic seals we use for our machines _____ salt water, oil, and acids.*	detect
	extract
b. fasten together; put together: *Next week the engineers will _____ the two parts of the bridge together.*	insert
	join
c. say we will do a certain thing: *I _____ to sell the secondhand car to you.*	promise
	resist
d. put something in: *First you must _____ the rivets into the pre-drilled holes.*	
e. discover something: *She could _____ no sign of rust when she examined the machine components.*	
f. obtain something (substances, etc.) by pressing, cooking, or some other process: *Many different processes are used to _____ iron from ore.*	

26 X-ray tire inspection

1 **Please read this text and "What's new on the market?" in lesson twenty-six ...**

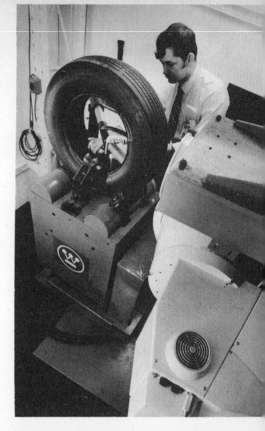

This view from inside the lead-lined room of a Westinghouse STX-400 tire inspection system shows the tire pedestal on the left, the X-ray source positioned inside the tire, and the X-ray television camera on the right. The entire body of the tire can be inspected by rotating the tire in different positions (the pedestal turns to allow this) to alternately expose the tread and both sidewalls to the camera. The part of the pedestal holding the tire can be raised or lowered to enable testing of different sizes of tires.

... and answer the following questions:

a. What do the TV pictures show?
b. What are the X-rays picked up by after passing through the tire?
c. What is used to line the walls?
d. Why should the tires be rotated on the pedestal?
e. Why is the operator in a different room?
f. Why can the part of the pedestal holding the tire be raised or lowered?
g. Where is the X-ray source positioned when testing starts?
h. What are the X-rays changed into?

2 Please put in "again", "all", "further", "often", "over", "some" or "very":

New words and phrases:
view [vju:] Ansicht; Bild; Aussicht
pedestal ['pedistl] Sockel; Podest
position in die richtige Stellung bringen; (ein)stellen
inspect [in'spekt] untersuchen; prüfen
the pedestal turns der Sockel läßt sich drehen
alternately wechselweise; abwechselnd
enable testing [i'neibl] (das) Testen ermöglichen
angry ['æŋgri] ärgerlich; zornig
hammer ['hæmə] Hammer; hämmern
chair ['tʃɛə] Stuhl; Sessel
a pair of pliers ['plaiəz] eine (Draht-, Kneif-)Zange
boy [bɔi] Junge
apprentice [ə'prentis] Auszubildender, Lehrling
bet [bet] wetten

a. If you have any _____ questions, please phone our representative in London. b. He was _____ angry when he heard that the machine had not been delivered on schedule. c. There were _____ tools lying on the chair in the corner: a hammer, _____ screwdrivers, a pair of pliers, and a small wrench. d. Is that boy _____ there a drilling machine operator, too? – No, he's one of our apprentices. e. Computers are _____ used to produce technical drawings. f. CAD is _____ valuable for storing _____ the information that has to be used _____ later on. g. She wasn't interested at _____. h. I'll have to go to Birmingham _____ next week. i. Under normal driving conditions, light pedal pressure is _____ that is needed to pull up safely in a short distance. j. Before we start with production, we should get _____ information from the chief engineer. k. How _____ do these buses run? – Every five minutes, I think. l. That company has produced _____ of the finest machine tools I've ever seen. m. That's _____ nice of you.

3 Please translate:

a. Er hat mir gestern gesagt, daß er gerne Ingenieur werden möchte. b. Unter normalen Fahrbedingungen hätte ich keine Schwierigkeiten gehabt. c. Wenn Sie mich gefragt hätten, hätte ich Ihnen die Computerdaten gegeben.

"I bet you can't guess which of us is the robot!"

27 Mathematical signs, symbols and operations

1 Please use the correct mathematical signs:

a. square root of *a* plus *b*: _____ **b.** six cubed: _____ **c.** X to the power of minus one times X cubed: _____ **d.** ten to the power of minus six: _____ **e.** twelve to the power of six: _____

2 Please find the correct explanation for the words on the right, and then put the words into the gaps in the sentences:

a. cause to come together at a central point: *The laser beam is picked up by a fresnel lens and _____ ed into a TV pick-up system.*	explode
	fix
b. get something started; begin: *They will _____ a new scheme aimed at helping disabled motorists;* set in motion: *NASA will _____ a rocket next month.*	fix
	focus
c. burst with a loud noise: *When the boiler _____ d, many people were injured by the steam.*	launch
	launch
d. use a cutting tool with sharp teeth along the edge of a thin, flat steel blade: *John has to _____ some boards in his workshop because he wants to build a shelf.*	saw
e. fasten something so that it cannot be moved: *Tomorrow he will _____ the shelf on the wall;* (besonders US:) put in order or repair: *We'll have to _____ the engine first before we do anything else.*	

3 Please put in "at", "for", "in", "into" or "of":

a. Some _____ the simulation models that have been developed eliminate the need _____ destructive tests. **b.** Although there was no lack _____ material, we were not able to repair the machines because _____ a strike. **c.** _____ specified time intervals, drawings can be obtained. **d.** Many _____ the tests necessary _____ vehicle safety are destructive _____ nature. **e.** The structural data are fed _____ a computer.

> **New words and phrases:**
>
> **explode** [iks'pləud] explodieren; sprengen
> **fix** [fiks] befestigen; festmachen; *(besonders US:)* reparieren
> **saw** sägen
> **burst** [bə:st] (burst – have burst) platzen; bersten
> **sharp** [ʃa:p] scharf
> **teeth** [ti:θ] (Mehrzahl von tooth [tu:θ] Zähne
> **et last** [ət 'la:st] endlich; schließlich
> **lack** [læk] Mangel; Fehlen
> **there was no lack of ...** es fehlte nicht an ...
> **because of ...** wegen ...
> **strike** Streik

4 The mathematical sign for ...

a. "indefinitely great" is _____ (symbol of infinity). **b.** pi (the number 3.14159265+) is _____. **c.** "is equal to", "equals" is _____. **d.** "is greater than" is _____

5 Please fill in the gaps by putting in the correct abbreviations:

a. tin _____
b. newton _____
c. nano _____
d. manganese _____
e. lead _____
f. number _____
g. decibel _____
h. gallon _____
i. joule _____
j. ounce _____
k. feet _____

G. SHERMAN

28 NASA: Projects in space...

1 Please put in the following words:

> billion, come, contain, million, recommend, reduce, requirements

Atmosphere. The space colony's atmosphere was designed to _____ the same amount of oxygen as on earth but with slightly less than half as much nitrogen, so that the total atmospheric pressure would be about half that at sea level on earth.

Radiation shielding. Away from the earth's magnetic field cosmic radiation is intense. The scientists _____ that radiation exposure should be reduced by shielding to a level that is equivalent to the US standard for the general population. The ten _____ tons of shielding required to _____ exposure in the space colony below this level would _____ from the slag from processed ore.

Cost of project. On the basis of the _____ the environment places on engineering, the total price of the colony, including all the development work leading towards it, is likely to be about $100 _____, between two and three times the cost of the Apollo project.

2 Please put in "allow", "get", "keep/kept", "leave" or "let":

a. You ought to _____ the leaflets translated before going to England. b. _____ me alone for a while, will you? I have to write a new computer programme. c. Although I had an appointment with him for eight o'clock, he _____ me waiting till a quarter to nine. d. Why didn't you use the machine tools? – Well, the foreman didn't _____ me to use them. e. Why don't you _____ him to go to Birmingham? – Because I need him here in the factory. f. Please _____ me know when the machine parts can be delivered. g. Please do your best to _____ the machine running. h. Don't _____ the lights on when you _____ the workshop this evening. i. We'll have to _____ the booster rockets re-designed before we can launch the spacecraft. j. Don't _____ your tool kit in the workshop when you go home.

New words and phrases:

atmospheric pressure [æt-məsˈferik] Luftdruck
shield abschirmen
shielding Abschirmung
cosmic radiation [ˈkɔzmik] Höhenstrahlung
intense [inˈtens] stark; intensiv
exposure [iksˈpəuʒə] Ausgesetztsein (Strahlungen oder anderen Einflüssen)
equivalent [iˈkwivələnt] gleichwertig; entsprechend
population [pɔpjuˈleiʃən] Bevölkerung
requirements [riˈkwaiəmənts] Anforderungen; Bedürfnisse
environment [inˈvaiərənmənt] Umgebung; Umwelt
darling [ˈdɑːliŋ] Liebling
dead [ded] tot
have your batteries gone dead? sind deine Batterien leer?
till [til] bis

3 Please translate:

a. Die NASA-Rakete ist gestern gestartet worden. b. Ja, ich habe es im Fernsehen gesehen. c. Glauben Sie, daß man eine Raumkolonie bauen wird? – In einigen Jahren sicher.

Life among the robots . . .

"Darling, you are so cold. Don't you like me or have your batteries gone dead?"

29 ...and progress on earth

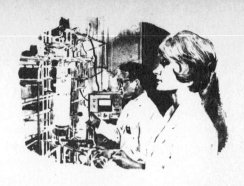

Please complete the text below and on the opposite page:

Scientific studies. The Space Shuttle is capable _____ taking _____ earth orbit completely equipped scientific laboratories manned _____ scientists, technicians, and engineers. _____ the weightless environment _____ space, researchers can perform many tasks that cannot be performed _____ earth.

Mineral resources. Large mineral deposits have been identified _____ many parts _____ the world as a result _____ Skylab photographs. The more sophisticated satellites launched _____ the Space Shuttle are expected _____ make many more valuable mineral discoveries. The data will be used _____ federal departments, industry, and colleges, _____ give just a few examples.

Environment. Satellites can send weather information _____ the ground, identify the sources _____ air and water pollution, and

This hypersonic transport model has been tested in wind tunnels at the Langley Research Center at speeds ranging from Mach 0.36 to 6.0.

29

monitor air quality. A suitably equipped satellite can cover the entire United States _____ about 500 photographs; cameras carried _____ high-altitude airplanes would use about 500,000 photographs _____ cover the same area. What would take years to monitor _____ air can be monitored _____ space _____ a few days.

Petroleum resources. Photographs _____ the earth taken _____ space have already supported explorations _____ oil and natural gas _____ the world. The improved satellites _____ the Space Shuttle years will be able _____ locate new sources _____ these fuels.

New words and phrases:

mineral ['minərəl] Mineral-; mineralisch
resources [ri'sɔːsiz] Reichtümer (eines Landes); Mittel
mineral resources Mineralvorkommen; Erzvorkommen
deposit [di'pɔzit] Vorkommen; Lager; Ablagerung, Schicht
identify [ai'dentifai] erkennen; identifizieren; feststellen
photograph ['fəutəgrɑːf] Foto(grafie), Bild
they are expected to make ... man erwartet, daß sie ... machen
discovery [dis'kʌvəri] Entdeckung
support unterstützen

Agriculture. Sensor systems _____ space can help the world solve its food problems. The sensors _____ the satellites will monitor the fields and can detect diseases and insects. The information obtained _____ this way will help the world's food experts calculate the total amount _____ food available throughout the world. These satellites will also be able _____ give early warnings _____ fire, send information _____ the construction _____ better maps, and generally make farm planning easier.

30 A digital watch kit

1 Please put in the following words:

> accuracy, assembly, chip, department, design, kit, letter, quartz, second, silicon, trimmer (2 ×), watch, year

a. The complete kit includes batteries, LED display, _____, chip, _____ crystal – in fact, nothing is lacking for easy _____.
b. The heart of the watch is a _____ of _____ that measures only 3 mm × 3 mm and contains over 2,000 transistors.
c. The chip is totally designed and manufactured in Great Britain, and it is the first _____ to include all the circuits necessary for a digital watch in a single chip.
d. You will be able to finish the _____ in just a few hours of work.
e. When I had some trouble and asked the Sinclair service _____ for help, they sent me a very kind and helpful _____.
f. When you assemble the _____ yourself, you may be able to adjust the _____ to achieve an _____ within a _____ a week.
g. A correctly-assembled watch is guaranteed for a _____. It works as soon as you put the batteries in.

LED display

Trimmer

Quartz crystal

Batteries

2000-transistor silicon integrated circuit

2 Please put in "whatever", "whenever" or "wherever":

a. Where shall I put the box with the rivets? – Oh, you can put it _____ you like. **b.** His workshop isn't very clean. _____ I looked, there were dirty tools lying around on the tables and workbenches. **c.** She goes to see her friends _____ she is in Birmingham. **d.** You can say _____ you like but I'm quite sure that aluminium would be much better for these components. **e.** You can give me a call and discuss it with me _____ you like. **f.** Keep calm, _____ happens.

New words and phrases:

trimmer ['trimə] Trimmer
lack fehlen
chip ['tʃip] Chip (= Halbleiterteilchen)
finish beenden; fertigstellen; (fertig) bearbeiten
kind freundlich; gütig
helpful hilfreich
accuracy ['ækjurəsi] Genauigkeit
whatever was (auch) immer; alles was
wherever wo(hin) auch immer; ganz gleich, wo(hin)
one thing's for sure eins ist sicher
tea trolley ['trɔli] Teewagen

30

"One thing's for sure – that tea trolley wasn't built here."

Final test

Part A – Choose the best answer in each case:

1 The temperature at which pure ice melts is ... **a.** $-10°C$. **b.** $0°C$. **c.** $+10°C$. **d.** $+32°C$.

2 What is missing from the following diagram of an energy conversion demonstration? **a.** battery **b.** generator **c.** meter **d.** pump **e.** switch

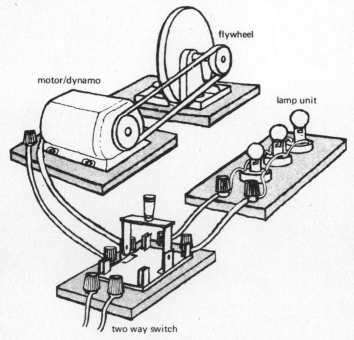

3 Sulphur is an example of ... **a.** a compound. **b.** a metal. **c.** a mixture. **d.** a sulphide. **e.** an element.

4 The least number of elements which can form a compound is ... **a.** 0. **b.** 1. **c.** 2. **d.** 3. **e.** 4.

5 Which of the following diagrams shows the correct arrangement of the lines of force produced by an electric current flowing through a coil of wire?

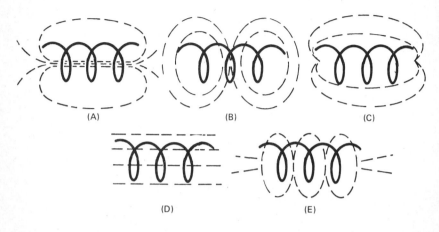

6 Look at the energy conversion set-up below. Choose a suitable comment. **a.** The bulb will not light very brightly. **b.** Why not connect the bulb directly to the battery? **c.** It must be a big battery to run all three things. **d.** The bulb may blow. **e.** The generator is charging the battery.

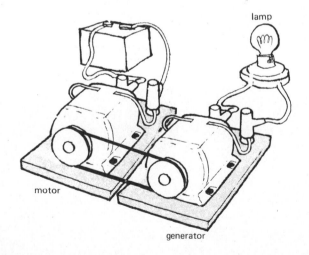

7 Which one is an insulator? **a.** knife blade **b.** penny **c.** plastic **d.** sheet of cooking foil **e.** silver spoon

8 Which of the following will be the best conductor? **a.** asbestos **b.** carbon **c.** glass **d.** iron **e.** plastic

9 Air is a mixture of . . . **a.** hydrogen, nitrogen, and carbon dioxide. **b.** hydrogen, oxygen, and carbon dioxide. **c.** hydrogen, oxygen, and nitrogen. **d.** oxygen, nitrogen, and carbon dioxide.

10 In the following sketches all the cells and lamps are similar. In which case will the lamp be brightest?

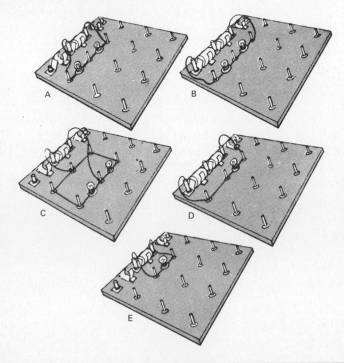

11 The two most common elements on the surface of the earth . . . **a.** iron and silicon. **b.** oxygen and iron. **c.** oxygen and aluminium. **d.** oxygen and silicon. **e.** silicon and aluminium.

12 In which of the following pieces of electrical apparatus is a diode used? **a.** dynamo **b.** electric cooker **c.** electric motor **d.** radio

13 Which of the following comments about electricity in the home is *false?* **a.** Different households require different amounts of electrical power. **b.** Electricity is sold in units of kilowatt hours. **c.** Fuses convert alternating current into direct current. **d.** Household applicances are connected in parallel. **e.** Mains electricity is alternating current.

14 Modern houses are often equipped with double-glazing because ... **a.** glass is a good conductor of heat. **b.** air trapped between the panes* prevents convection. **c.** radiation cannot pass through the air between the panes. **d.** radiation passes better through the trapped air. **e.** air trapped between the panes reduces conduction.

15 Which of the following comments is true? Hydrogen ... **a.** is lighter than air. **b.** is heavier than air. **c.** is soluble in water. **d.** supports combustion. **e.** does not burn.

16 The Bronze Age (bronze is an alloy of copper and tin) came before the Iron Age in history. Copper was probably discovered before iron because ... **a.** there are more copper compounds than iron compounds on the surface of the earth. **b.** Copper compounds need less energy to release the copper. **c.** copper compounds are usually nearer to the earth's surface.

17 Heating coal in a limited supply of air gives a material commonly used in industry for obtaining metals from their ores. This material is ... **a.** coal gas. **b.** coke. **c.** sodium. **d.** sulphur. **e.** tar

18 A thermometer measures ... **a.** heat. **b.** expansion. **c.** temperature. **d.** weather.

19 In which unit is pressure measured? **a.** ampere **b.** newton **c.** watt **d.** pascal **e.** lumen

---

* pane [pein] = (Fenster-)Scheibe

20 The abbreviation for "tungsten" is . . . **a.** Tu. **b.** St. **c.** W.

21 The sketch shows a battery connected by a single wire to a lamp. The lamp will not light because . . . **a.** the wire is too thin. **b.** the wire is too long. **c.** the wire may be broken inside the insulation. **d.** there is no switch in the diagram. **e.** there is no return path.

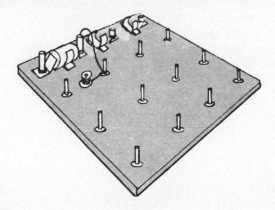

22 In the following lighting circuit there is one faulty connecting wire. Lamp L_1 lights but L_2 and L_3 are out. Where is the break?

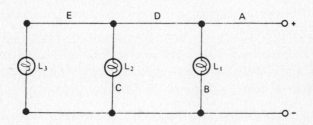

23 A body moves in one direction at constant speed. If no force is applied the body will . . . **a.** change its direction. **b.** change its shape. **c.** continue at the same speed. **d.** slow down. **e.** speed up.

24 Which of the following is the unit for measuring force? **a.** joule **b.** kilogram **c.** newton **d.** pascal **e.** pound

Part B – Which is the correct answer?

25 The first car produced on an assembly line was Ford's T Model _____ rolled through the factory gates four times faster than rival products.
 a. what
 b. which
 c. who

26 The costs of telephone calls will be even lower when the Shuttle takes new and improved satellites _____ earth orbit.
 a. at
 b. for
 c. into

27 Powered by solid propellants, the booster rockets will _____ have about 2.5 million pounds of thrust.
 a. each
 b. every
 c. every one

28 The Apollo explorations have shown that lunar materials contain from 20 to 30 per cent metals, 20 per cent silicon and 40 per cent oxygen _____ weight.
 a. at
 b. by
 c. in

29 The Westinghouse X-ray tire inspection system shows breaks in cords and _____ in the rubber.
 a. faults
 b. mistakes

30 In certain situations, pneumatically powered tools are preferable, _____ for instance where there is the danger of fire or explosion.
 a. as
 b. such
 c. thus

31 The new hypersonic transport model has been tested in wind tunnels at speeds _____ from Mach 0.36 to Mach six.
 a. developing
 b. ranging
 c. spreading

32 In the new plant General Motors built for the Vega, five railway tracks _____ straight into the factory, carrying steel and components.
 a. go
 b. going
 c. that go

33 Until now, repair and servicing costs of front-wheel drive cars have generally been higher than _____ of simple rear-wheel drive cars.
 a. such
 b. those
 c. which

34 The new car has disc brakes in the front and drum brakes _____ the rear.
 a. at
 b. in

71

Schlüssel zu den Übungen und zum Test

LESSON 1

1 **Nr. 13:** another; **Nr. 14:** same; **Nr. 16:** necessary; **Nr. 17:** attractive; **Nr. 18:** single; **Nr. 20:** faster; **Nr. 21:** economically

2 **a.** got used; **b.** get used; **c.** get used; **d.** used; **e.** used; **f.** got used; **g.** get used; **h.** got used

3 **a.** And how many (spark plugs) did she buy? **b.** Where is he from? **c.** How did he manage that? **d.** And why wasn't he interested? **e.** And why is she going (to London)?

LESSON 2

1 **a.** of ... about ... of; **b.** without; **c.** to ... after ... with ... in ... by; **d.** With ... of ... in; **e.** to ... to

2 **a.** talk ... know; **b.** told ... attend; **c.** have used; **d.** found; **e.** have prevented

3 **a.** have done; **b.** do; **c.** did; **d.** Did ... did ... did ... do ... have done; **e.** did

LESSON 3

1 **a.** MV (= megavolts) ... km ... m ... ft ... km; **b.** MW (= megawatts) ... bbl (= barrels)

2 **a.** But drilling platforms are often built in dry docks (*oder:* ... in a dry dock). **b.** But aluminium is often used for window frames. **c.** But cross-over networks are often included in loudspeaker kits (*oder:* ... a cross-over network is often used ...). **d.** But machine parts are often covered with a paint finish. **e.** But computers are often used for such jobs (*oder:* But a computer is ...).

3 **a.** –; **b.** to; **c.** – ... –; **d.** –

4 **a.** what; **b.** which; **c.** which; **d.** what; **e.** what; **f.** which; **g.** what

LESSON 4

1 *Electrical resistance ...:* **a.**); *A resistor is used to ...:* **b**); *Wow is ...:* **b**); *An integrated circuit is ...:* **b**); *Soldering means ...:* **a**); *Hertz (abbreviation Hz) is an SI unit which indicates ...:* **a**)

2 a. She wanted to know what I needed the leaflets for.   **b.** He asked me whether there would be any practical work.   **c.** She wanted to know why I didn't study electronics at home.   **d.** He wanted to know whether (*oder:* if) I was interested in a new loudspeaker.   **e.** She asked me what I had to learn for my fundamental electronics course.
3 a. to;   **b.** for;   **c.** in;   **d.** in

LESSON 5

1 *How do I replace burned-out lights? 1.:* assembly ... 1; *2.:* 2; *3.:* fluorescent ... 3 ... 13 ... shops; *What is that three-bladed fan at the top?* stirrer ... cavity ... 140 ... rotation ... interior; *How much faster is microwave cooking than conventional cooking?* speed ... kind ... meat ... items; *Will I damage my microwave oven if I turn it on empty?* tube ... finish
2 a. = W;   **b.** = R;   **c.** = W;   **d.** = W
3 a. – ... – ... –;   **b.** The ... –;   **c.** –
4 a. What's the technician doing? – He's repairing the motor. – How long **has he been** repairing it now? – **For** almost an hour.   **b.** What's Joan doing? – She's waiting **for** the chief engineer. – How long **has she been waiting** for him now? – **Since** eight o'clock.   **c.** What's the chief engineer doing? – **He's checking** the new milling machine. – How long has he been checking it now? – **For** half an hour.   **d.** What's Mr Eaton doing in the workshop? – He's talking to the technicians. – How long **has he been talking** to them? – **Since** he came to the office at nine o'clock this morning.   **e.** What's Jeff doing? – He's programming the computer. – **How long has he been programming the computer (now)?** – **Since** early this morning.

LESSON 6

1 a. rolled edge;   **b.** compression ... nylon;   **c.** outward flow
2 a. have been living (*oder:* have lived);   **b.** have you known;   **c.** have you been waiting;   **d.** have not seen;   **e.** have always wanted (*oder:* always wanted) ... have never been
3 a. about   **b.** of;   **c.** about;   **d.** for ... for;   **e.** for
4 a. much;   **b.** many ... much;   **c.** many

LESSON 7

1 a. replied;   **b.** called;   **c.** approved;   **d.** handle;   **e.** got;   **f.** investigate;   **g.** returned;   **h.** typed
2 a. to;   **b.** on;   **c.** On;   **d.** in;   **e.** in ... of

LESSON 8

1 a. = inlet (*oder:* intake); **b.** = compressor; **c.** = fuel; **d.** = turbine; **e.** = air; **f.** = gear box; **g.** = propeller (*oder:* fan); **h.** = engine
2 a. that; **b.** that . . . if; **c.** which; **d.** which (*oder:* that); **e.** when; **f.** which
3 a. I can't check the lift fan. You'll have to get it checked by somebody else, I'm afraid. **b.** I can't type the minutes. You'll have to get them typed by somebody else, I'm afraid. **c.** I can't explain the conveyor system. You'll have to get it explained by somebody else, I'm afraid. **d.** I can't translate the English leaflets. You'll have to get them translated by somebody else, I'm afraid. **e.** I can't repair the gas turbine. You'll have to get it repaired by somebody else, I'm afraid.
4 a. had been; **b.** was; **c.** had been; **d.** had been; **e.** was; **f.** had been

LESSON 9

1 *Accessories. Mobile power microphone:* regular . . . right . . . extra; *Telephone handset:* convenient . . . Great . . . noisy; *Desk power microphone:* integrated . . . 800; *Power speaker:* noisy / *Specifications:* 23 . . . $2\frac{1}{4}$ . . . 5.5 . . . 0.7 . . . 3
2 a. for the (*oder:* out for) . . . on; **b.** for; **c.** over; **d.** by . . . on; **e.** for
3 a. whose; **b.** who; **c.** whose; **d.** whose; **e.** who; **f.** who; **g.** who

LESSON 10

1 b. = air conditioning; **c.** = generator; **d.** = pump; **e.** = passenger; **f.** = hydraulic
2 a. The engineer I showed the machine to last Tuesday is very efficient. **b.** The operator I talked to yesterday is from Birmingham. **c.** The man I met in Pasadena is a policeman. **d.** The driver who told me about the restaurant yesterday is still in London. **e.** The woman I told you about this morning is a student.
3 a. who; **b.** –; **c.** who; **d.** who; **e.** –
4 a. lb (*oder:* pounds); **b.** on

LESSON 11

1 Across: 1 vibration; 4 car; 8 Co; 9 rust; 11 rotary; 13 Mn; 14 valves; 16 km; 17 ha; 22 acceleration. **Down:** 2 bus; 3 tires; 5 ac; 6 roadsign; 7 hr; 9 road; 10 tank; 12 ASA; 14 VA; 15 lb; 18 AA; 19 Al; 20 Pa; 21 Si

2 a. I told him yesterday that he must (*oder:* will have to) repair the machine as soon as possible. **b.** When do you want to (*oder:* are you going to) install the air-conditioning unit (*oder:* system)? – Next week, probably. (*Oder:* Probably next week.) **c.** You should have told him that he needs a paper disc for this experiment. **d.** You should get the car washed when you are at the garage. **e.** Did he tell you that we will be getting (*oder:* are getting) a new computer? – Yes, I talked to him yesterday. **f.** If I had known that the car has such a high petrol consumption I certainly wouldn't have bought it. **g.** You needn't get (*oder:* have) the letter translated. **h.** You should have read the operating instructions first.
3 a. but ... so (*oder:* as); **b.** as; **c.** as; **d.** than

LESSON 12

1 a. the ... the ... – ... the ... –; **b.** the ... the ... the; **c.** the ... the; **d.** –; **e.** –; **f.** (the) ... the; **g.** the
2 a. kind; **b.** way; **c.** way; **d.** way
3 a. up; **b.** on; **c.** together; **d.** for; **e.** about; **f.** to (*oder:* with); **g.** on

LESSON 13

1 a. Although they had made ... **b.** When (*oder:* While) Mr Hindshaw was talking ... (*Oder:* Mr Hindshaw was talking to his men when ...) **c.** When the buckled section ... **d.** When Jack Hindshaw arrived ... **e.** Jack Hindshaw called his men to the lift but again he was too late.
2 collapse = **e.**; crash = **f.**; fear = **a.**; fit = **c.**; hoist = **g.**; join = **h.**; melt = **d.**; remove = **l.**; span = **j.**; supply = **i.**; tremble = **k.**
3 a. for; **b.** at; **c.** in ... to ... for; **d.** on; **e.** to ... down; **f.** on; **g.** in; **h.** on ... into (*oder:* in); **i.** down ... on

LESSON 14

1 Solution: The plane will leave without you. You had to drive at an average speed of 60 miles per hour for the ten-mile trip. This means that you only had ten minutes in which to make the whole trip. If you drive the first five miles at an average speed of 30 miles per hour, you have already used up the ten minutes.
2 A1 + B3; A2 + B5; A3 + B6; A4 + B1; A5 + B4; A6 + B2
3 a. does; **b.** would; **c.** to
4 a. travelling; **b.** to say; **c.** mind
5 a. in; **b.** On ... in; **c.** in

LESSON 15

1 **Solution (second "computer game"):** SHELL OIL
2 **a.** of; **b.** to ... at ... to; **c.** to ... into (*oder:* in); **d.** from ... for ... on ... off ... for; **e.** with (*oder:* and)
3 **a.** Not only the manager is interested in (the) new computers. **b.** Not only the politicians are worried about the future. **c.** Not only Joan is afraid of getting seasick. **d.** Not only the technicians are looking forward to the holidays. **e.** Not only Jack is trying to get admitted to college.
4 **a.** I don't mind if he goes to England. (*Oder:* I don't mind his going to England.) **b.** Why have you changed your mind? – Well, I find the new solution better. **c.** She has made up her mind to accept the position (*oder:* job) in the USA. **d.** Do you mind if I use the computer? (*Oder:* Do you mind my using the computer?) – No, certainly not. (*Oder:* No, not at all.)
5 **a.** do; **b.** do; **c.** do; **d.** make

LESSON 16

1 **a.** mandrel ... action; **b.** rivet ... steel; **c.** component ... hole; **d.** machine ... tail ... head. *Richtige Reihenfolge:* Bild 3 + **c.**; Bild 1 + **d.**; Bild 4 + **a.**; Bild 2 + **b.**
2 **a.** Blind ... usually; **b.** really efficient; **c.** apart ... main ... increasingly; **d.** usually ... considerable; **e.** especially valuable
3 **a.** none; **b.** no ... no; **c.** not; **d.** No, not; **e.** none; **f.** no; **g.** none

LESSON 17

1 **Solution:** Two minutes.
2 aerosol = **b.**; bumper = **e.**; crucible = **c.**; die = **f.**; foundry = **g.**; mandrel = **a.**; tread = **d.**
3 **a.** wasn't he? **b.** doesn't it? **c.** did he? **d.** shouldn't he?
4 **a.** that (*oder:* which); **b.** one; **c.** will; **d.** one
5 **a.** –; **b.** –; **c.** –; **d.** the; **e.** the

LESSON 18

1 Maximum speed: 276 mph at sea level, **267** mph at an altitude of **10,000** ft / Range at 10,000 ft altitude: **585** miles with a 20-minute reserve / Take-off distance: **1,800** ft / wing span: **17** ft / Length: **12.4** ft / Height: **6** ft / Fuel capacity: **55** gal / Empty weight: **450** lbs / Gross weight: **960** lbs

2 **a.** very; **b.** very; **c.** very much; **d.** very
3 **a.** every ... even; **b.** ever; **c.** ever; **d.** even
4 to a small extent = **c.**; off the main road = **a.**; take them away = **a.**; it's far from easy = **b.**; get admitted to college = **b.**; nothing but trouble = **c.**; he failed to understand = **b.**; who is in charge = **b.**; it's virtually maintenance-free = **a.**
5 **a.** Why didn't you go (*oder:* drive) to England last week? – I had to write the new computer programmes first. **b.** If you want to assemble the BD-5J jet, you will need some machine tools. **c.** Some people have been waiting for weeks for the approval of the Federal Aviation Agency. **d.** The new pocket calculator has a built – in vocabulary of 24 words. **e.** If you had asked the chief engineer, these difficulties wouldn't have come up. **f.** There are not many riveting machines which have such a high efficiency. **g.** Have you ever been to New Mexico? – Yes, I spent my holiday there two years ago.

LESSON 19

1 **a.** serious (*oder:* right) ... often; **b.** practical ... head-on ... grey; **c.** easy ... several ... few ... very ... painted ... right; **d.** interesting ... possible ... little
2 **a.** Well, we would have used it if we had known how to program(me) it. **b.** Well, we would have carried it out if we had had some fuse wire. **c.** Well, we would have repaired it if we had had a new mandrel. **d.** Well, we would have bought it if we had had enough money. **e.** Well, we would have assembled it ourselves if we had had some machine tools.
3 **a.** such; **b.** so; **c.** such; **d.** so; **e.** so
4 **a.** as; **b.** only ... into; **c.** of ... set; **d.** All the ... to

LESSON 20

1 We are seeking qualified draughtsmen **with** a number **of** years experience **in** the field **of** steam generation plant **for** (*oder:* in) ships. You will be involved **in** the preparation **of** drawings **for** our own works and **for** subsidiaries throughout Europe and **in** the USA. We can offer plenty **of** variety **in** this specialised field, **with** excellent prospects **for** (*oder:* of) promotion and a good salary. Our benefits package includes profit share, free lunches, and generous holidays. Assistance **with** accommodation can also be arranged. **For** further information, including details **of** salary and benefits, please write **to** ...
2 **a.** each ... every; **b.** each; **c.** every; **d.** every; **e.** each; **f.** each
3 **a.** Well, I would have got it tuned if I'd had enough time to go to the workshop. **b.** Well, I would have got it installed if the technician hadn't been on holiday.

c. Well, I would have got it translated if I'd had someone who can translate letters into English. **d.** Well, I would have got it checked if I'd had a good technician. **e.** Well, I would have got it assembled if the machine tools hadn't been out of order. **f.** Well, I would have got them replaced if I'd had new ones. **g.** Well, I would have got it washed if the garage hadn't been closed. **h.** Well, I would have got it repaired if I'd had the necessary spare parts.

LESSON 21

1 a. invested; **b.** all; **c.** as ... costs; **d.** as ... as; **e.** be ... without; **f.** be ... lower

2 Engine (**957** cc) / Bore **74** mm / Stroke **55.7** mm / Compression ratio **8.3** : 1 / Maximum torque at **2,700** rpm 64 Nm / Ratio **18.62** to 1 / Turning circle **9.3** m

3 a. well; **b.** good; **c.** fine; **d.** well; **e.** good; **f.** well; **g.** well; **h.** well; **i.** good; **j.** well

LESSON 22

2 a. = W; **b.** = R; **c.** = W; **d.** = R; **e.** = R; **f.** = R; **g.** = W

3 he's not likely to come = **a.**; without extra charge = **b.**; they should pool their money = **c.**; on schedule = **c.**; you ought to make up your mind = **a.**

LESSON 23

1 A1 + B6; A2 + B2; A3 + B3; A4 + B4; A5 + B1; A6 + B5

2 a. just; **b.** just; **c.** only; **d.** only (*oder:* just); **e.** only; **f.** just; **g.** just

3 a. easily ... be careful; **b.** added ... threads; **c.** fall below ... with; **d.** range

4 a. Instead of going to Birmingham, she went to London. **b.** Instead of writing the letter, she wrote the minutes. **c.** Instead of saying "here you are", she said "please". **d.** Instead of visiting the foundry, she visited the car factory. **e.** Instead of buying an electric heater, she bought a solar panel system. **f.** Instead of using steel for the machine parts, she used aluminium. **g.** Instead of testing the Fiesta, she tested the Jaguar XJ-S.

5 a. would; **b.** will; **c.** Neither; **d.** can; **e.** Neither

LESSON 24

1 *Illustration numbers:* 13/20/5+6/1/3/2/9/17/18/8/16/12/10/11/7/4/15/14/19

2 a. up; **b.** through; **c.** out; **d.** on; **e.** of

3 a. k = kilogram(me); **b.** N = Newton; **c.** LCD = liquid-crystal display; **d.** VTOL = vertical take-off and landing; **e.** J = joule; **f.** ppm = parts per million; **g.** R & D = research and development; **h.** O. H. C. = overhead camshaft; **i.** Cu = cuprum (copper); **j.** C = carbon; **k.** Fe = ferrum (iron); **l.** Sb = stibium (antimony); **m.** bhp = brake horsepower; **n.** Pa = Pascal; **o.** no = number; **p.** STOL = short take-off and landing; **q.** rad = radian; **r.** LED = light-emitting diode; **s.** HD = heavy duty; **t.** bbl = barrels; **u.** deg = degree; **v.** rev/min = revolutions per minute

LESSON 25

1 a. use ... power; **b.** allow ... crawl; **c.** last; **d.** unplug; **e.** install; **f.** cut; **g.** connect
2 a. Should the electronic equipment need to be repaired, the modules can easily be replaced. **b.** Should the oil level need to be checked, the dipstick can easily be inserted. **c.** Should the circulation pump need to be controlled, a temperature switch can easily be installed. **d.** Should the liquid need to be transported, a pipe line can easily be built.
3 a. its; **b.** It's ... it's
4 a. on; **b.** for ... to ... through; **c.** on ... of
5 a. = resist; **b.** = join; **c.** = promise; **d.** = insert; **e.** = detect; **f.** = extract

LESSON 26

1 a. They show the insides of tire treads and sidewalls. **b.** They are picked up by an X-ray amplifier and a TV camera. **c.** Lead. **d.** So that tread and the sidewalls can be alternately exposed to the camera. **e.** To protect him (or her) from the X-rays. **f.** To enable testing of different sizes of tires. **g.** Inside the tire. **h.** Light rays.
2 a. further; **b.** very; **c.** some ... some; **d.** over; **e.** often; **f.** very (*oder:* often) ... all ... again; **g.** all; **h.** again; **i.** all; **j.** further; **k.** often; **l.** some; **m.** very
3 a. He told me yesterday that he would like to be (*oder:* become) an engineer. **b.** Under normal driving conditions I would not have had any trouble (*oder:* any difficulties). **c.** If you had asked me I would have given you the computer data.

LESSON 27

1 a. $\sqrt{a+b}$ **b.** 6^3 **c.** $\chi^{-1} \cdot \chi^2$ **d.** 10^{-6} **e.** 12^6
2 a. = focus; **b.** = launch; **c.** = explode; **d.** = saw; **e.** = fix
3 a. of ... for; **b.** of ... of; **c.** At; **d.** of ... for ... in; **e.** into
4 a. ∞ **b.** π **c.** = **d.** >
5 a. Sn; **b.** N; **c.** n; **d.** Mn; **e.** Pb; **f.** no; **g.** db; **h.** gal; **i.** J; **j.** oz; **k.** ft

LESSON 28

1 *Atmosphere:* contain; *Radiation shielding:* recommend ... million ... reduce ... come; *Cost of project:* requirements ... billion
2 a. get; **b.** Leave; **c.** kept; **d.** allow; **e.** allow; **f.** let; **g.** get (*oder:* keep); **h.** leave ... leave; **i.** get; **j.** leave
3 a. The NASA rocket was launched yesterday. **b.** Yes, I saw (*oder:* watched) it on television. **c.** Do you think a space colony will be built? (*Oder:* Do you think they will build ...?) – In a few years (*oder:* some years' time), certainly.

LESSON 29

Scientific studies: of ... into ... by ... In ... of ... on
Mineral resources: in ... of ... of ... by ... to ... by ... to
Environment: to ... of ... with ... by (*oder:* in) ... to ... by ... from ... in
Petroleum resources: of ... from ... of ... around (*oder:* throughout) ... of ... to ... of
Agriculture: in ... in ... in ... of ... to ... of ... for ... of

LESSON 30

1 a. trimmer ... quartz ... assembly; **b.** chip ... silicon; **c.** design; **d.** kit (*oder:* watch); **e.** department ... letter; **f.** watch (*oder:* kit) ... trimmer ... accuracy ... second; **g.** year
2 a. wherever; **b.** Wherever; **c.** whenever; **d.** whatever; **e.** whenever; **f.** whatever

FINAL TEST

Part A

1 = b.; **2** = a.; **3** = e.; **4** = c.; **5** = (A); **6** = b.; **7** = c.; **8** = d.; **9** = d.; **10** = D; **11** = d.; **12** = d.; **13** = c.; **14** = e.; **15** = a.; **16** = b.; **17** = b.; **18** = c.; **19** = d.; **20** = c.; **21** = e.; **22** = the break is at D; **23** = c.; **24** = c.

Part B

25 = b.; **26** = c.; **27** = a.; **28** = b.; **29** = a.; **30** = a.; **31** = b.; **32** = a.; **33** = b.; **34** = a.

Alphabetisches Wortschatzregister

Die Zahlen verweisen auf die Lektion, in der das Wort in einer bestimmten Bedeutung zum erstenmal vorkommt.

about 23
abroad 13
accuracy 30
accurately 17
aerosol 17
affect 25
air intake 8
all the way through 1
alternately 26
analyse 12
angry 26
appear 5
apprentice 26
at last 27
atmospheric 28
attention 19
away 14
awfully 4

back and forth 11
back 12
baffle 24
because of 27
bet 26
blade 5
boa constrictor 19
board 23
boiler 20
book 20
bore 21
brake pad 21
breather tube 24
but (nothing but) 18
button 9

cap screw 24
cast 17

catch a plane 14
certain 2
character 2
chair 26
chamber 21
chauffeur 13
chip 30
circle 21
circuit 4
circular 11
clamp 16
clear 12
collision 14
combination 21
combustion 21
come up 15
compression ratio 21
connector 24
considerable 5
contact 17
controlled 6
convenient 9
cosmic 28
cover 24
crane 12
crankcase 24
cross 18

dark 19
darling 28
date 16
dead 28
deposit 29
desk 9
diagonal 21
die 17
digit 15
discovery 29
drunken 19

each 20
edge 6
emission 21
enable 26
end 24
exhaust emission 21
extent 2
enclosure 7
environment 28
equivalent 28
expect 29
explode 27
explosive 14
exposure 28
extend 13
extensive 22

fall in 13
fan 5
file 7
film 4
finish 30
fire 6
fix 27
flow 6
fluorescent (light) 5
fluorspar 12
for sure 30
force 6
forge 17
forth 11
freeway *(US)* 19
fuel inlet 8
fumes 14

gap 25
girl 19
glow 19
go over something 1

grass 19
greatly 22
ground roll 18

hammer 26
handset 9
head 24
head-on 19
helpful 30
hexagon 24
hit 23
humidity 10

ideal 2
identical 10
identify 29
ill 20
impedance 9
impurities 12
increase 11
increasingly 16
industrial 22
inlet 8
input 9
inspect 26
inspection 21
instant(ly) 23
intake 8
intense 28
investigate 7
invoice 22
iron oxide 12

joint 16
journalist 19

keep away 14
kind 30

81

knot 8
know-how 3

lack 27, 30
ladle 12
landing distance 18
last (at last) 27
lay 3
lift-up 13
lifting fan 8
lime 12
list 24
load 18
lunch 20

mail 7
mathematics 14
microphone 9
mid range 2
mineral 29
minor 23
mostly 8
mould 17
move 6
Ms 14

nominal 10
nothing but 18

obtain 25
obvious 23
on schedule 22
on time 14
operate 1
order 20
ore 25
out of order 20
output 9
outward 6
overhead 12
oxide 12

pack 17
package 20
packing 1
pad 21
pair 26
parts list 24
pass 12
pass on 7
pay attention 19
pedestal 26
photograph 29
pick 15
pinion 21
pleasure 13
pliers 26
plug 23
pocket 15
pool 22
population 28
position 26
power range 2
preamplifier 9
precise 23
preparation 20
pressure-proof 6
prevention 19
promotion 20
public way 11
punch 15
pure 10

rack and pinion 21
radiation 28
range 2, 18
rating 10
ratio 21
receiver 9
recoil 23
reddish-brown 11
reinforced 3
relative(ly) 23
release 17
reproduce 2, 17
requirements 28
reserve 18
residential 22
resources 29

retainer 24
rim 11
rod 17
roll 6, 18
run 14, 21

schedule 22
score 23
sensitivity 9
separate 2
sequence 16
shape 17
share 20
sharp 27
shield 28
ship 9
short circuit 4
shutdown 24
simplify 16
simulate 23
single 1
skirt 3
smooth 1
sober 19
socket head cap
  screw 24
somehow 6
sound range 2
south 22
span 18
speaker 9
specialized 20
split 21
spray 17
stamp 17
stand 14
strike 27
stroke 21
style 24
subsidiary 20
substance 17
summer 22
supplier 1
support 29
sure (for sure) 30
swing back 12
swing clear 12

take off 12
take-off distance 18
tap 12
taste 19
tea trolley 30
teeming ladle 12
thermal 22
BTU 22
tight 16
till 28
to a certain extent 2
tonnage 12
torque 21
transport 3
transmittal 7
trimmer 30
trolley 30
troubleshooter 14
trust 2
tube connector 24
turn 15, 17, 21, 26

unaffected 25
undercarriage 10
unlike 12
useful load 18
utilize 3

via 10, 23
vibration 6
view 26
volume control 15

washer 24
way 1, 11
wear 21
wedge 21
weight 9
whatever 30
wherever 30
widely 12
wing span 18
working pool 22
works 20

Erklärung der Lautschrift

[ʌ]	kurzes *a*, etwa wie in dt. m*a*tt	bus [bʌs]
[ɑ:]	langes *a*, etwa wie in dt. l*a*hm	car [kɑ:]
[ai]	etwa wie in dt. E*i*s, f*ei*n	right [rait]
[au]	etwa wie in dt. Fr*au*, H*au*s	brown [braun]
[æ]	mehr zum *a* hin als dt. *ä* in W*ä*sche	back [bæk]
[e]	kurzes *e*, wie in dt. B*e*tt	men [men]
[ei]	nicht wie in dt. *Ei*, sondern *e-i*, d. h. von [e] zu [i] gleiten	plate [pleit]
[ɛə]	*ä* wie in dt. B*ä*r, dann zu [ə] gleiten	where [wɛə]
[ə]	kurzes, unbetontes *e*, etwa wie in dt. grüß*e*n, bitt*e*	matter ['mætə]
[ə:]	etwa wie in dt. K*ö*rner (aber ohne *r*!)	girl [gə:l]
[əu]	von [ə] zu [u] gleiten	no [nəu]
[i]	kurzes *i*, etwa wie in dt. m*i*t	it [it]
[i:]	langes *i*, etwa wie in dt. n*ie*, L*ie*be	see [si:]
[iə]	von kurzem *i* zu [ə] gleiten	here [hiə]
[ɔ]	kurzes offenes *o*, etwa wie in dt. G*o*tt	not [nɔt]
[ɔ:]	langes offenes *o*, etwa wie in dt. K*o*rn	all [ɔ:l]
[ɔi]	etwa wie in dt. n*eu*	boy [bɔi]
[u]	kurzes *u*, etwa wie in dt. M*u*tter	book [buk]
[u:]	langes *u*, etwa wie in dt. Sch*uh*	who [hu:]
[uə]	kürzer als in dt. K*ur*	sure [ʃuə]

[ŋ]	wie in dt. la*ng*e	young [jʌŋ]
[r]	nicht rollen! Zunge an den Gaumen und leicht zurückbiegen	round [raund]
[s]	wie in dt. rei*ß*en, wi*ss*en	Miss [mis]
[z]	wie in dt. rei*s*en, le*s*en	please [pli:z]
[θ]	wie *ß* in dt. Fa*ß*, aber gelispelt, d. h. Zunge an obere Vorderzähne	both [bəuθ]
[ð]	wie *s* in dt. *s*att, aber gelispelt, d. h. Zunge an obere Vorderzähne	that [ðæt]
[ʃ]	wie in dt. Ti*sch*	fresh [freʃ]
[ʒ]	wie in dt. Gara*g*e, Lo*g*e	television ['teliviʒn]
[v]	wie in dt. *W*ein, *V*ioline, *V*isum	visit ['vizit]
[w]	nicht wie dt. *w*! Mit vorgestülpten Lippen gebildetes kurzes *u*, von dem man schnell zum nachfolgenden Laut übergleitet	well [wel]

[:]	bedeutet, daß der vorangehende Laut lang gesprochen wird	who [hu:]
[']	steht vor der betonten Silbe	about [ə'baut]

Quellenverzeichnis

Wir danken den nachstehenden Personen, Publikationen, Firmen und Institutionen, daß sie uns den Nachdruck von Text- und Bildmaterial in der vorliegenden Form gestattet haben.

Die arabischen Ziffern verweisen auf die Lektionen, die römischen auf die Seiten der jeweiligen Lektion (z. B. 14/I = Lektion 14, 1. Seite).

Airbus Industrie (Paris) 10/I (Illustrationen und Text)
A.L.I. Press Agency (Brüssel) 6/II, 7/II, 15/II, 26/II, 28/II (Illustrationen)
British Hovercraft Corporation (East Cowes, Isle of Wight) 8/I (Illustrationen)
British Steel Corporation (England) 12/I (Illustrationen und Text), 12/II (Illustrationen)
Cleveland Institute of Electronics, Inc. (Cleveland, Ohio) 4/I (Illustration unten links)
Design Engineering (London) 6/I (Illustration)
Economist (London) 2. Umschlagseite (Diagramm aus Measurement Guide)
Electronics Technical Institute (Little Falls, New Jersey) 4/I (Illustration oben rechts)
Engineers' Digest (London) 16/I (Illustration)
Engineering (Design Council, London) 1/I (Illustration und Text)
Erich Pabel Verlag (München) 28/I (Illustration)
Evening News (London) 10/II (Illustration)
Guns & Ammo (Los Angeles, California) 23/I (Illustration)
Heinemann (London) Final Test, Items 2, 5, 6, 10, 21, 22 (aus Science for the 70's by A. J. Mee, Patricia Boyd, David Ritchie)
Høyer-Ellefsen (Oslo) 3/I (Text)
Hy-Gain Electronics Corporation (Lincoln, Nebraska) 9/I (Illustration und Text)
Ingersoll-Rand Co. Ltd. (London) 24/I (Illustration und Text)
Lüning, Werner (Lübeck) 2/I (Illustration oben rechts), 2/II, 4/II, 11/II, 13/II, 14/II, 16/II, 17/II, 30/II (Illustrationen)
Milwaukee Journal (Milwaukee, Wisconsin) 19/I (Illustration und Text)
Motor (London) 21/I, 21/II (Illustrationen)
NASA – National Aeronautics and Space Administration 22/I (Illustrationen und Text), 28/I (Text), 29/I, 29/II (Illustrationen und Text)
National Bureau of Standards (Washington) 3. Umschlagseite (Illustrationen)
Norris Industries (Los Angeles, California) 5/I (Illustrationen und Text)
Parade Publications (New York) 27/II (Illustration)
Pioneer Electronics (Tokio) 2/I (Illustrationen und Text)
Punch → Lüning, Werner
Scottish Education Department (Edinburgh) Final Test, Items 2, 5, 6, 10, 21, 22 (Reproduced from material prepared by the Working Party on Secondary School Science, by permission of the Scottish Education Department)
Shell U. K. Exploration and Production (London) 3/I (Illustration)
Sherman, G. (St. Petersburg, Florida) 27/II (Illustration)
Sinclair Radionics Ltd. (St. Ives, Huntingdon) 30/I (Illustration)
VDI Nachrichten (Düsseldorf) 24/II (Illustration)
Westinghouse Electric Corporation (Pittsburgh, Pennsylvania) 26/I (Illustration und Text)
Wuschak, G. (Düsseldorf) 24/II (Illustration)